M000046256

Applying the Word to Human Problems & Issues

A TOPICAL BIBLE REFERENCE GUIDE FOR CHRISTIAN COUNSELORS & LEADERS

Emmanuel Ahia

TRILOGY CHRISTIAN PUBLISHERS

TUSTIN, CA

Trilogy Christian Publishers

A Wholly Owned Subsidiary of Trinity Broadcasting Network

2442 Michelle Drive

Tustin, CA 92780

Manufactured in the United States of America

10 9 8 7 6 5 4 3 2 1

Library of Congress Cataloging-in-Publication Data is available.

ISBN: 978-1-64773-278-3

E-ISBN: 978-1-64773-279-0

Contents

Preface & Acknowledgements

In the last two decades, there has been a rapid increase of professional counseling agencies as a result of expanded licensure and certification regulations for mental health professionals. These regulations have created opportunities for appropriately credentialed professionals to access financial sources that were previously unavailable to them. All fifty states now have laws that govern the training and practice of counseling, leading to insurance coverage and payment for Licensed Professional Counselors (LPC) who now account for one third of the mental health care workforce.

This trend includes professional Christian counseling agencies that may or may not be affiliated to any Christian denomination. To access insurance payments, counselors in faith-based or church-affiliated counseling centers must be trained and licensed in accordance with their respective state laws and regulations. Sometimes, this leads to divided loyalties and lack of balance between Christian and secular counseling. This is not to say that they are inherently mutually exclusive.

More and more, "professional Christian counselors" working even in Christian agencies, are concerned more about secular issues and principles than they are of Christian principles. Many have become oblivious about what the Bible teaches concerning a counseling subject matter or clients' presenting problems. Sometimes, what the Bibles teaches is totally ignored. The point here is not that state-approved counselor training and licensure requirements are inappropriate for Christian counseling. Rather that counseling without adequate understanding and application of what the Bible teaches about mental health presenting problems such as alcoholism, drugs, physical and sexual abuse/exploitation, anger, anxiety, divorce, death and dying, marriage, stress, etc., should not be considered as Christian counseling.

The best healing for a Christian experiencing life-challenging issues, can only come from a knowledge of what the Bible teaches and appropriate application of that word to the client's life and issues. Secular knowledge, born out of socio-psychological research can of course be useful but only when subordinated to the scriptures. For example, the generally accepted fact that about 80 percent of what people typically worry about never happens, is useful information for a Christian to know, but it should not be a substitute for what the Bible teaches about anxiety and fear. For the believer, the words and works of men, no matter how brilliantly articulated, cannot adequately achieve the same spiritual results because they are not spiritually designed. Psalms 1:1-3 is specific on this issue.

The first purpose of this book is to topically identify and itemize what the Bible says about many mental health-related issues often presented to pastors, counselors, lay counselors and other Christian leaders. The topical passages and verses cited are not comprehensive or exhaustive. Each counselor should continue to grow these topics and passages. Although just a single book, we know that the Bible is alive and so vast that no one book such as this can be exhaustive. Moreover, the Holy Spirit can show a Christian counselor a more appropriate passage to meet a client's need depending on the circumstance.

The second purpose is to help Christian counselors cultivate the interest and habit of recognizing and using Bible passages that relate to various mental health issues as they serve their clients. Thirdly, as Christian counselors, pastors, church leaders, and Bible teachers we are not immunized to the mental health issues that our clients and parishioners face. Knowledge of these passages and personally applying them to our own lives will help us maintain spiritual focus and resilience even as we serve the people of God. They help us to remain spiritually equipped.

I sincerely acknowledge the quick and dedicated help I received from Sister Donna Taylor during this venture. Her training, editing abilities, and love for God's work were indispensable to the quick completion of this guide. I further acknowledge the positive and prompt responsiveness of Sister Beth Cintron whenever there arose a need to move things along. Sisters Catherine Crawford and Kassandra Dauphin were both very helpful in identifying additional and appropriate Bible verses that were later included in the manuscript. For that, I also thank them. A noteworthy backdrop to all these, is our senior pastor David Farina, Sr., whose habitual encouragement of all who serve under him, is a constant in our ministry. I personally appreciate his examples, his devotion to his calling, and his unflinching loyalty to the Word of God.

Introduction

To understand and use this text appropriately, important fundamentals are necessary. First, God can use human understanding and skills to bring healing and wholeness to a client or a parishioner, but He does not depend on them. He can always bring healing, wholeness, and peace to the life of human beings through His word or a miraculous intervention. If the user does not truly believe in the supernatural power of God to intervene in human problems and issues, he or she may not benefit the most from the use of the text.

Second, the role of a true Christian counselor is ambassadorial. They represent and present God's Word through love and compassion to suffering and lost humanity. It is this commitment and identity that helps the counselor filter appropriate secular training and skills needed for meeting the need for any mental health client. This role implies a dependency on the Lord and the Holy Spirit, developing listening skills that show Christian love and nonjudgmental concern or a presence and attention that makes a client feel accepted as Christ would.

In addition, authentic Christian counselors should have an elevated sense of self-awareness. This helps them serve effectively even when they are going through their own personal issues. The ultimate result will be that clients' care will not be jeopardized. Attitudes such as impulsivity and impatience are inconsistent with Christian virtues and therefore unacceptable. It can be said that the practice of confidentiality is the opposite of gossip which is not a Christian virtue.

With the above said, the user will find the following steps useful.

- *Understand the client spiritually.* Some clients may or may not know the Lord. Others may either be mature or babies in Christ. These facts will determine where and how you should proceed with a client.

- *Understand the problem specifically by answering these questions:* What exactly is the pain, loss, desire, guilt, etc.? How does this affect the person's life? What does he or she consider to be the source of the problem? Did he or she play any role in causing the problem? What does the person see as the solution(s) to the problem?

- *Move from problem to solution by addressing these questions:* How old or new is the problem/issue (chronicity)? What solutions have he or she tried? What are the bases for the choice of solutions? Who else is involved with him or her in working on the solutions? How helpful have the solutions been? What other solutions have they considered?

- *Understand what the Bible teaches about the problem or issue and Bible characters who have experienced this or an identical problem.* For example, Job experienced great suffering, Joseph experienced great injustice, and Hanna experienced childlessness.

- *What Bible virtues may be helpful for the resolution of the issues?* Examples are faith, honesty/truthfulness, prayerfulness, hope, forgiveness, love, courage, patience, perseverance, humility, etc.

- *Remember to be a good steward of your clinical mental healthcare training.* God can use it for the ultimate good of your clients.

- *Remember that even when a client's issue appears to be purely secular, there may in fact exist a spiritual dimension to it.*

Abandonment/ Rejection

- When a person is feeling that no one cares or is asking, "Where is my God?"
- When a person is feeling rejected by loved ones.
- God himself never abandons His people.
- He always restores His people whenever they repent of their sins and come back to Him.

And the LORD, He is the One who goes before you. He will be with you, He will not leave you nor forsake you; do not fear nor be dismayed.

—Deuteronomy 31:8

He shall deliver you in six troubles, Yes, in seven no evil shall touch you.

—Job 5:19

When my father and my mother forsake me, Then the LORD will take care of me.

—Psalms 27:10

But I will sing of Your power; Yes, I will sing aloud of Your mercy in the morning; For You have been my defense, And refuge in the day of my trouble.

—Psalms 59:16

For the LORD will not cast off His people, nor will He forsake His inheritance.

—Psalms 94:14

Can a woman forget her nursing child, and not have compassion on the son of her womb? Surely, they may forget, Yet I will not forget you.

—Isaiah 49:15

Through the LORD's mercies we are not consumed, Because His compassions fail not. They are new every morning; Great is Your faithfulness. "The LORD is my portion," says my soul, "Therefore I hope in Him! " The LORD is good to those who wait for Him, To the soul who seeks Him.

—Lamentations 3:22–25

I am the good shepherd. The good shepherd gives His life for the sheep. But a hireling, he who is not the shepherd, one who does not own the sheep, sees the wolf coming and leaves the sheep and flees; and the wolf catches the sheep and scatters them. The hireling flees because he is a hireling and does not care about the sheep. I am the good shepherd; and I know My sheep and am known by My own.

—John 10:11–14

What then shall we say to these things? If God is for us, who can be against us?

—Romans 8:31

But the Lord is faithful, who will establish you and guard you from the evil one.

—2 Thessalonians 3:3

And when the Chief Shepherd appears, you will receive the crown of glory that does not fade away.

—1 Peter 5:4

NOTES:

Abortion

- For abortion counseling and Christian education
- Use for restoration and reconciliation of clients to the Lord.
- Do not use verses for condemnation or passing judgement.
- Judgement belongs to the Lord; He still loves sinners and can save them.
- Believers should not use ungodly means to try to stop this ungodly behavior.

You shall not murder.

—Deuteronomy 5:17

Only be sure that you do not eat the blood, for the blood is the life; you may not eat the life with the meat.

—Deuteronomy 12:23

Behold, children are a heritage from the Lord, the fruit of the womb is a reward.

—Psalms 127:3

For You formed my inward parts; You covered me in my mother's womb. I will praise You, for I am fearfully and wonderfully made; Marvelous are Your works, and that my soul knows very well. My frame was not hidden from You, When I was made in secret, and skillfully wrought in the lowest parts of the earth. Your eyes saw my substance, being yet unformed. And in Your book, they all were written, the days fashioned for me, when as yet there were none of them.

—Psalms 139:13-16

NOTES:

Aging

- The importance of staying close to God at any age and at all times
- Use to encourage people to seek the Lord at any age, especially in their youth.

The days of our lives are seventy years; And if by reason of strength they are eighty years, yet their boast is only labor and sorrow; For it is soon cut off, and we fly away. So teach us to number our days,
That we may gain a heart of wisdom.
—Psalms 90:10,12

Sing praises to the LORD, who dwells in Zion! Declare His deeds among the people.
—Psalms 91:16

For by me your days will be multiplied, and years of life will be added to you.
—Proverbs 9:11

Remember now your Creator in the days of your youth, Before the difficult days come, And the years draw near when you say, "I have no pleasure in them" While the sun and the light, the moon and the stars, are not darkened, and the clouds do not return after the rain. In the day when the keepers of the house tremble, and the strong men bow down; When the grinders cease because they are few, and those that look through the windows grow dim. When the doors are shut in the streets, And the sound of grinding is low; When one rises up at the sound of a bird, and all the daughters of music are brought low. Also, they are afraid of height, and of terrors in the way; When the almond tree blossoms, the grasshopper is a burden, and desire fails. For man goes to his eternal home, And the mourners go about the streets. Remember your Creator before the silver cord is loosed, Or the golden bowl is broken, Or the pitcher shattered at the fountain, Or the wheel broken at the well. Then the dust will return to the earth as it was, And the spirit will return to God who gave it. "Vanity of vanities," says the Preacher, "All is vanity."

—Ecclesiastes 12:1–8

NOTES:

EMMANUEL AHIA

Alcohol, Drugs, and Other Addictions

- Christ can set us free from all addictions that enslave us and dishonor Him.
- He sets captives free.

Wine is a mocker, Strong drink is a brawler, and whoever is led astray by it is not wise.

—Proverbs 20:1

Therefore if the Son makes you free, you shall be free indeed.

—John 8:36

But the fruit of the Spirit is love, joy, peace, longsuffering, kindness, goodness, faithfulness, gentleness, self-control. Against such there is no law.

—Galatians 5:22–23

And do not be drunk with wine, in which is dissipation; but be filled with the Spirit,

—Ephesians 5:18

NOTES:

Anger

- Useful for spiritual counseling and understanding of anger.
- Anger should never be used to justify violence or other sins.
- It is never good to make decisions when you are angry.
- Prolonged anger and bitterness are self-destructive.
- Pray about your anger and seek God's help for resolution of the causes.
- Anger can lead to unforgiveness.
- Unforgiveness always displeases the Lord.

A soft answer turns away wrath, but a harsh word stirs up anger.

—Proverbs 15:1

"Be angry, and do not sin": do not let the sun go down on your wrath, nor give place to the devil.

—Ephesians 4:26–27

Let all bitterness, wrath, anger, clamor, and evil speaking be put away from you, with all malice.

—Ephesians 4:26–27

But now you yourselves are to put off all these: anger, wrath, malice, blasphemy, filthy language out of your mouth.
—Colossians 3:8

So then, my beloved brethren, let every man be swift to hear, slow to speak, slow to wrath; for the wrath of man does not produce the righteousness of God.

—James 1:19–20

NOTES:

Anxiety/Fear

- For helping clients/ believers understand the futility of anxiety when we trust in the Lord.
- Walking with the Lord dispels anxiety and fear.
- Believers need not to be afraid or anxious even when they are not immediately seeing the results of thier trust in Him.
- The only time a believer should worry is when he/she places his/her trust in man instead of on the Lord.

Then all this assembly shall know that the LORD does not save with sword and spear; for the battle is the LORD's, and He will give you into our hands.

—1 Samuel 17:47

Yea, though I walk through the valley of the shadow of death, I will fear no evil; For You are with me; Your rod and Your staff, they comfort me.

—Psalms 23:4

I sought the LORD, and He heard me, and delivered me from all my fears.

—Psalms 34:4

Therefore, we will not fear, even though the earth be removed, and though the mountains be carried into the midst of the sea; Though its waters roar and be troubled, Though the mountains shake with its swelling. Selah There is a river whose streams shall make glad the city of God, The holy place of the tabernacle of the Most High.

—Psalms 46:2–4

In the multitude of my anxieties within me, Your comforts delight my soul.

—Psalms 94:19

The LORD is on my side;
I will not fear. What can man do to me?

—Psalms 118:6

It is vain for you to rise up early, to sit up late, to eat the bread of sorrows; For so He gives His beloved sleep.

—Psalms 127:2

Anxiety in the heart of man causes depression, but a good word makes it glad.

—Proverbs 12:25

Say to those who are fearful-hearted, "Be strong, do not fear! Behold, your God will come with vengeance, With the recompense of God; He will come and save you."

—Isaiah 35:4

But now, thus says the LORD, who created you, O Jacob, And He who formed you, O Israel: "Fear not, for I have redeemed you; I have called you by your name; You are Mine.

—Isaiah 43:1

Therefore, do not worry about tomorrow, for tomorrow will worry about its own things. Sufficient for the day is its own trouble.

—Matthew 6:34

But take heed to yourselves, lest your hearts be weighed down with carousing, drunkenness, and cares of this life, and that Day come on you unexpectedly.

—Luke 21:34

Peace I leave with you, My peace I give to you; not as the world gives do I give to you. Let not your heart be troubled, neither let it be afraid.

—John 14:27

Be anxious for nothing, but in everything by prayer and supplication, with thanksgiving, let your requests be made known to God; and the peace of God, which surpasses all understanding, will guard your hearts and minds through Christ Jesus. Finally, brethren, whatever things are true, whatever things are noble, whatever things are just, whatever things are pure, whatever things are lovely, whatever things are of good report, if there is any virtue and if there is anything praiseworthy—meditate on these things.

—Philippians 4:6–8

For God has not given us a spirit of fear, but of power and of love and of a sound mind.

—2 Timothy 1:7

Casting all your care upon Him, for He cares for you.
—1 Peter 5:7

NOTES:

Backsliding

- It is God's will that we always maintain our relationship with Him.
- He is always waiting to forgive us, cleanse us of our sins, and reconcile us to Himself.

The backslider in heart will be filled with his own ways, but a good man will be satisfied from above.
—Proverbs 14:14

Let the wicked forsake his way, And the unrighteous man his thoughts; Let him return to the LORD, And He will have mercy on him; And to our God, For He will abundantly pardon.
—Isaiah 55:7

for you are still carnal. For where there are envy, strife, and divisions among you, are you not carnal and behaving like mere men?
—1 Corinthians 3:3

Therefore, He is also able to save to the uttermost those who come to God through Him, since He always lives to make intercession for them.

—Hebrews 7:25

If we confess our sins, He is faithful and just to forgive us our sins and to cleanse us from all unrighteousness.

—1 John 1:9

Nevertheless, I have this against you, that you have left your first love. Remember therefore from where you have fallen; repent and do the first works, or else I will come to you quickly and remove your lampstand from its place—unless you repent.

—Revelation 2:4–5

NOTES:

Baptism

- After people are saved (born again), they need water baptism as a testimony to the world of their salvation.
- The practice of water baptism for those who have not personally accepted Christ is not scriptural.

Go therefore and make disciples of all the nations, baptizing them in the name of the Father and of the Son and of the Holy Spirit,

—Matthew 28:19

Therefore, remember that you, once Gentiles in the flesh— who are called Uncircumcision by what is called the Circumcision made in the flesh by hands—that at that time you were without Christ, being aliens from the commonwealth of Israel and strangers from the covenants of promise, having no hope and without God in the world. But now in Christ Jesus you who once were far off have been brought near by the blood of Christ.

—Ephesians 2:11–13

In Him you were also circumcised with the circumcision made without hands, by putting off the body of the sins of the flesh, by the circumcision of Christ, buried with Him in baptism, in which you also were raised with Him through faith in the working of God, who raised Him from the dead.

—Colossians 2:11–12

NOTES:

Bitterness

- We were forgiven and saved so that we can forgive others and reconcile them to the Lord.
- Bearing grudges and wishing that evil befall others is ungodly.
- Interpersonal bitterness cannot coexist with forgiveness.
- When unbelievers do us wrong, it presents us an opportunity to lead them to Christ by forgiving them.
- We must always remember that the Lord can forgive those who have wronged us if they confess that wrong to Him. If He forgives them, He will protect them from our bitterness.

For if you forgive men their trespasses, your heavenly Father will also forgive you. But if you do not forgive men their trespasses, neither will your Father forgive your trespasses.
—Matthew 6:14–15

Bless those who persecute you; bless and do not curse. Rejoice with those who rejoice, and weep with those who weep. Be of the same mind toward one another. Do not set your mind on high things but associate with the humble. Do not be wise in your own opinion. Repay no one evil for evil. Have regard for good things in the sight of all men. If it is possible, as much as depends on you, live peaceably with all men. Beloved do not avenge yourselves, but rather give place to wrath; for it is written, "Vengeance is Mine, I will repay," says the Lord. Therefore, "If your enemy is hungry, feed him; If he is thirsty, give him a drink; For in so doing you will heap coals of fire on his head." Do not be overcome by evil but overcome evil with good.

—Romans 12:14–21

Let all bitterness, wrath, anger, clamor, and evil speaking be put away from you, with all malice.

—Ephesians 4:31

looking carefully lest anyone fall short of the grace of God; lest any root of bitterness springing up cause trouble, and by this many become defiled.

—Hebrews 12:15

But if you have bitter envy and self-seeking in your hearts, do not boast and lie against the truth. This wisdom does not descend from above, but is earthly, sensual, demonic.

—James 3:14–15

Who, when He was reviled, did not revile in return; when He suffered, He did not threaten, but committed Himself to Him who judges righteously.

—1 Peter 2:23

NOTES:

Bondage

- See "Alcohol & Drugs"

Wine is a mocker, Strong drink is a brawler, and whoever is led astray by it is not wise.

—Proverbs 20:1

And you shall know the truth, and the truth shall make you free.

—John 8:32

Then the Lord knows how to deliver the godly out of temptations and to reserve the unjust under punishment for the day of judgment,

—2 Peter 2:9

NOTES:

Child Abuse

- Child abuse is against the law and against moral uprightness.
- Laws against child abuse must be obeyed by everybody, especially Christians.
- Disciplining a child in love is not child abuse (See "Parenting").

Let every soul be subject to the governing authorities. For there is no authority except from God, and the authorities that exist are appointed by God. Therefore, whoever resists the authority resists the ordinance of God, and those who resist will bring judgment on themselves. For rulers are not a terror to good works, but to evil. Do you want to be unafraid of the authority? Do what is good, and you will have praise from the same.

—Romans 13:1–3

And everyone who competes for the prize is temperate in all things. Now they do it to obtain a perishable crown, but we for an imperishable crown. Therefore, I run thus: not with uncertainty. Thus, I fight not as one who beats the air. But I discipline my body and bring it into subjection, lest, when I have preached to others, I myself should become disqualified.

—1 Corinthians 9:25–27

And you, fathers, do not provoke your children to wrath, but bring them up in the training and admonition of the Lord.

—Ephesians 6:4

Therefore, submit yourselves to every ordinance of man for the Lord's sake, whether to the king as supreme, or to governors, as to those who are sent by him for the punishment of evildoers and for the praise of those who do good.

—1 Peter 2:13–14

NOTES:

Courage

- Christian confidence and courage are evidence that we trust the Lord of Hosts and we are relying on the guiding power of the Holy Spirit.
- It also shows that we remember His mighty works and miracles on behalf of His people from generation to generation.

Have I not commanded you? Be strong and of good courage; do not be afraid, nor be dismayed, for the Lord your God is with you wherever you go.

—Joshua 1:9

Wait on the Lord; Be of good courage, And He shall strengthen your heart; Wait, I say, on the Lord!

—Psalms 27:14

"Yet now be strong, Zerubbabel," says the Lord; "and be strong, Joshua, son of Jehozadak, the high priest; and be

strong, all you people of the land," says the Lord, "and work; for I am with you," says the Lord of hosts.

—Haggai 2:4

NOTES:

EMMANUEL AHIA

Covetousness/
Envy/Jealousy

- Envy is sinful and shows that we are not content / satisfied with God's provision for us His people.
- Envy is always a tool in the devil's hand. It drags us backwards spiritually
- Envy can cause us to commit other sins.

You shall not covet your neighbor's house; you shall not covet your neighbor's wife, nor his male servant, nor his female servant, nor his ox, nor his donkey, nor anything that is your neighbor's.

—Exodus 20:17

Do not fret because of evildoers, nor be envious of the workers of iniquity.

—Psalms 37:1

Hatred stirs up strife, but love covers all sins.

—Proverbs 10:12

For he knew that they had handed Him over because of envy.

—Matthew 27:18

And do this, knowing the time, that now it is high time to awake out of sleep; for now our salvation is nearer than when we first believed. The night is far spent; the day is at hand. Therefore, let us cast off the works of darkness, and let us put on the armor of light. Let us walk properly, as in the day, not in revelry and drunkenness, not in lewdness and lust, not in strife and envy. But put on the Lord Jesus Christ, and make no provision for the flesh, to fulfill its lusts.

—Romans 13:11–14

for you are still carnal. For where there are envy, strife, and divisions among you, are you not carnal and behaving like mere men?

—1 Corinthians 3:3

Let us not become conceited, provoking one another, envying one another.

—Galatians 5:26

Therefore, laying aside all malice, all deceit, hypocrisy, envy, and all evil speaking, as newborn babes, desire the pure milk of the word, that you may grow thereby

—1 Peter 2:1–2

NOTES:

Criticism/
Judgmental

- Useful verses to encourage personal reflection when a person is being consumed by the failures and shortcomings of others.
- It is poor evidence of Christian maturity if we habitually criticize others rather than pray for them.
- We ought to use the scripture to teach, correct, rebuke, and for "training in righteousness" rather than criticism.

And why do you look at the speck in your brother's eye, but do not consider the plank in your own eye? Or how can you say to your brother, "Let me remove the speck from your eye"; and look, a plank is in your own eye? Hypocrite! First remove the plank from your own eye, and then you will see clearly to remove the speck from your brother's eye.

—Matthew 7:3–5

Judge not, and you shall not be judged. Condemn not, and you shall not be condemned. Forgive, and you will be forgiven.

—Luke 6:37

There is therefore now no condemnation to those who are in Christ Jesus, who do not walk according to the flesh, but according to the Spirit...Who is he who condemns? It is Christ who died, and furthermore is also risen, who is even at the right hand of God, who also makes intercession for us.

—Romans 8:1,34

Therefore, let him who thinks he stands take heed lest he fall.

—1 Corinthians 10:12

Examine yourselves as to whether you are in the faith. Test yourselves. Do you not know yourselves, that Jesus Christ is in you? —unless indeed you are disqualified.

—2 Corinthians 13:5

NOTES:

Death

- Useful for helping people understand that death is not the end of human life. It is the beginning of eternal life.
- God has the final say about both death and after death. God's judgment will follow.
- Because believers will spend eternity with Christ, we should not grieve like those who do not know Him.

For I know that my Redeemer lives, And He shall stand at last on the earth; And after my skin is destroyed, this I know, that in my flesh I shall see God, Whom I shall see for myself, and my eyes shall behold, and not another. How my heart yearns within me!

—Job 19:25–27

He will swallow up death forever, And the Lord God will wipe away tears from all faces; The rebuke of His people He will take away from all the earth; For the Lord has spoken.

—Isaiah 25:8

O Death, where is your sting? O Hades, where is your victory?

—1 Corinthians 15:55

And as it is appointed for men to die once, but after this the judgment

—Hebrews 9:27

NOTES:

Death (Grieving After a Person Dies)

- Death is only the end of this earthly life; it is the gateway to eternity with the Lord or with the devil in hell.
- Because believers will spend eternity with Christ, we should not grieve like those who do not know the Lord.
- Shouldn't this cause believers to witness more for Christ?

And he said, "While the child was alive, I fasted and wept; for I said, 'Who can tell whether the Lord will be gracious to me, that the child may live?' But now he is dead; why should I fast? Can I bring him back again? I shall go to him, but he shall not return to me."

—2 Samuel 12:22–23

Jesus said to her, "I am the resurrection and the life. He who believes in Me, though he may die, he shall live."

—John 11:25

Let not your heart be troubled; you believe in God, believe also in Me. In My Father's house are many mansions; if it were not so, I would have told you. I go to prepare a place for you. And if I go and prepare a place for you, I will come again and receive you to Myself; that where I am, there you may be also.

—John 14:1-3

For we know that if our earthly house, this tent, is destroyed, we have a building from God, a house not made with hands, eternal in the heavens. For in this we groan, earnestly desiring to be clothed with our habitation which is from heaven, if indeed, having been clothed, we shall not be found naked. For we who are in this tent groan, being burdened, not because we want to be unclothed, but further clothed, that mortality may be swallowed up by life. Now He who has prepared us for this very thing is God, who also has given us the Spirit as a guarantee. So we are always confident, knowing that while we are at home in the body we are absent from the Lord. For we walk by faith, not by sight. We are confident, yes, well pleased rather to be absent from the body and to be present with the Lord.

Therefore, we make it our aim, whether present or absent, to be well pleasing to Him.

—2 Corinthians 5:1–9

For to me, to live is Christ, and to die is gain.

—Philippians 1:21

But I do not want you to be ignorant, brethren, concerning those who have fallen asleep, lest you sorrow as others who have no hope. For if we believe that Jesus died and rose again, even so God will bring with Him those who sleep in Jesus. For this we say to you by the word of the Lord, that we who are alive and remain until the coming of the Lord will by no means precede those who are asleep. For the Lord Himself will descend from heaven with a shout, with the voice of an archangel, and with the trumpet of God. And the dead in Christ will rise first. Then we who are alive and remain shall be caught up together with them in the clouds to meet the Lord in the air. And thus, we shall always be with the Lord. Therefore comfort one another with these words.

—1Thessalonians 4:13–18

NOTES:

Debt

- Financial indebtedness reveals the true character of people.
- Believers ought not fall into debt as a result of wants or a fleshly desire to compete with others (see "Dissatisfaction/ Contentment").

The wicked borrows and does not repay, But the righteous shows mercy and gives.

—Psalms 37:21

The rich rules over the poor, And the borrower is servant to the lender.

—Proverbs 22:7

Owe no one anything except to love one another, for he who loves another has fulfilled the law.

—Romans 13:8

NOTES:

Depression

- Useful verses for helping people look to and rely on the Lord in times of existential pain, sickness, disappointments and/or trauma.
- Consult a psychiatrist if the depression persists, it may be "clinical" in nature.

Why are you cast down, O my soul? And why are you disquieted within me? Hope in God, for I shall yet praise Him For the help of His countenance. O my God, my soul is cast down within me; Therefore, I will remember You from the land of the Jordan, And from the heights of Hermon, From the Hill Mizar.

—Psalms 42:5-6

Come to Me, all you who labor and are heavy laden, and I will give you rest. Take My yoke upon you and learn from Me, for I am gentle and lowly in heart, and you will find rest for your souls. For My yoke is easy and My burden is light.

—Matthew 11:28-30

Not only that, but we also who have the first fruits of the Spirit, even we ourselves groan within ourselves, eagerly waiting for the adoption, the redemption of our body.

—Romans 8:23

In everything give thanks; for this is the will of God in Christ Jesus for you.

—1 Thessalonians 5:18

NOTES:

Desires (of the Flesh)

- Useful verses for reminding Christians the importance of being filled and guided by the Holy Spirit.
- A spirit-filled desire helps a person maintain a lifestyle that glorifies God.
- Spirit-directed desires make it possible for God to answer our prayers.
- A spirit-guided desire helps us determine and comply with God's will for our lives.

I say then: Walk in the Spirit, and you shall not fulfill the lust of the flesh.

—Galatians 5:16

You ask and do not receive, because you ask amiss, that you may spend it on your pleasures.

—James 4:3

Do not love the world or the things in the world. If anyone loves the world, the love of the Father is not in him. For all that is in the world--the lust of the flesh, the lust of the eyes, and the pride of life--is not of the Father but is of the world. And the world is passing away, and the lust of it; but he who does the will of God abides forever.

—1 John 2:15–17

NOTES:

Dissatisfaction/ Contentment

- Useful verses for helping people distinguish needs from and wants.
- Also, useful when encouraging a lifestyle of godly contentment.

Not that I speak regarding need, for I have learned in whatever state I am, to be content: I know how to be abased, and I know how to abound. Everywhere and in all things, I have learned both to be full and to be hungry, both to abound and to suffer need. I can do all things through Christ who strengthens me.

—Philippians 4:11–13

Now godliness with contentment is great gain. For we brought nothing into this world, and it is certain we can carry nothing out. And having food and clothing, with these we shall be content.

—1 Timothy 6:6–8

Let your conduct be without covetousness; be content with such things as you have. For He Himself has said, "I will never leave you nor forsake you. "So we may boldly say: "The Lord is my helper; I will not fear. What can man do to me?"

—Hebrews 13:5–6

NOTES:

Divorce

- These verses show the will of God about divorce.
- They should be used to counsel and educate believers against easy divorce.
- Believers should not divorce just because it is recommended by a secular counselor.

But I say to you that whoever divorces his wife for any reason except sexual immorality causes her to commit adultery; and whoever marries a woman who is divorced commits adultery.

—Matthew 5:32

The Pharisees also came to Him, testing Him, and saying to Him, "Is it lawful for a man to divorce his wife for just any reason?" And He answered and said to them, "Have you not read that He who made them at the beginning 'made them male and female,' and said, 'For this reason a man shall leave his father and mother and be joined to his wife, and the two shall become one flesh'? So then, they are no longer two but one flesh. Therefore, what God has joined together, let not man separate. "They said to Him, "Why then did Moses command to give a certificate of divorce, and to put her away?" He said to them, "Moses, because of the hardness of your hearts, permitted you to divorce your wives, but from the beginning it was not so. And I say to you, whoever divorces his wife, except for sexual immorality, and marries another, commits adultery; and whoever marries her who is divorced commits adultery."

—Matthew 19:3–9

Therefore, what God has joined together, let not man separate."

—Mark 10:9

Let the husband render to his wife the affection due her, and likewise also the wife to her husband. The wife does not have authority over her own body, but the husband does. And likewise, the husband does not have authority over his own body, but the wife does.

—1 Corinthians 7:3–4

Now to the married I command, yet not I but the Lord: A wife is not to depart from her husband. But even if she does depart, let her remain unmarried or be reconciled to her husband. And a husband is not to divorce his wife. But to the rest I, not the Lord, say: If any brother has a wife who does not believe, and she is willing to live with him, let him not divorce her. And a woman who has a husband who does not believe, if he is willing to live with her, let her not divorce him. For the unbelieving husband is sanctified by the wife, and the unbelieving wife is sanctified by the husband; otherwise your children would be unclean, but now they are holy. But if the unbeliever departs, let him depart; a brother or a sister is not under bondage in such cases. But God has called us to peace.

—1 Corinthians 7:10–15

Love suffers long and is kind; love does not envy; love does not parade itself, is not puffed up; does not behave rudely, does not seek its own, is not provoked, thinks no evil; does not rejoice in iniquity, but rejoices in the truth; bears all things, believes all things, hopes all things, endures all things.

—1 Corinthians 13:4–7

NOTES:

Doubt/Faith

- Faith in the Lord cannot coexist with doubt in His faithfulness and power to fulfill His promises to us.
- Without faith, it is impossible to please God.
- The just shall live by faith (see "Trusting in the Lord/Faith").

But immediately Jesus spoke to them, saying, "Be of good cheer! It is I; do not be afraid." And Peter answered Him and said, "Lord, if it is You, command me to come to You on the water. "So He said, "Come." And when Peter had come down out of the boat, he walked on the water to go to Jesus. But when he saw that the wind was boisterous, he was afraid; and beginning to sink he cried out, saying, "Lord, save me!" And immediately Jesus stretched out His hand and caught him, and said to him, "O you of little faith, why did you doubt?" And when they got into the boat, the wind ceased. Then those who were in the boat came and worshiped Him, saying, "Truly You are the Son of God."

—Matthew 14:27–33

So Jesus answered and said to them, "Assuredly, I say to you, if you have faith and do not doubt, you will not only do what was done to the fig tree, but also if you say to this mountain, 'Be removed and be cast into the sea,' it will be done."

—Matthew 21:21

But let him ask in faith, with no doubting, for he who doubts is like a wave of the sea driven and tossed by the wind. For let not that man suppose that he will receive anything from the Lord; he is a double-minded man, unstable in all his ways.

—James 1:6–8

NOTES:

Encouragement

- Useful for reassuring believers that the Lord will always "shepherd" them through the ups and downs of life.
- We have to trust Him for the above to happen.

The Lord is my shepherd; I shall not want. He makes me to lie down in green pastures; He leads me beside the still waters. He restores my soul; He leads me in the paths of righteousness For His name's sake. Yea, though I walk through the valley of the shadow of death, I will fear no evil; For You are with me; Your rod and Your staff, they comfort me. You prepare a table before me in the presence of my enemies; You anoint my head with oil; My cup runs over. Surely goodness and mercy shall follow me All the days of my life; And I will dwell in the house of the Lord Forever.

—Psalms 23:1–6

These things I have spoken to you, that in Me you may have peace. In the world you will have tribulation; but be of good cheer, I have overcome the world.

—John 16:33

My brethren, count it all joy when you fall into various trials, knowing that the testing of your faith produces patience. But let patience have its perfect work, that you may be perfect and complete, lacking nothing.

—James 1:2–4

NOTES:

Enemies

- Important verses for reminding believers that we do not "tit-for-tat" our enemies.
- The Holy Spirit can help us forgive our enemies and, by so doing, help them understand God's forgiveness.
- Vengeance belongs to the Lord (see "Vengeance").

If you meet your enemy's ox or his donkey going astray, you shall surely bring it back to him again If you see the donkey of one who hates you lying under its burden, and you would refrain from helping it, you shall surely help him with it.
—Exodus 23:4–5

Do not rejoice when your enemy falls, and do not let your heart be glad when he stumbles.
—Proverbs 24:17

But I say to you who hear: Love your enemies, do good to those who hate you, bless those who curse you and pray for those who spitefully use you. To him who strikes you on the one cheek, offer the other also. And from him who takes away your cloak, do not withhold your tunic either. Give to everyone who asks of you. And from him who takes away your goods do not ask them back. And just as you want men to do to you, you also do to them likewise. But if you love those who love you, what credit is that to you? For even sinners love those who love them. And if you do good to those who do good to you, what credit is that to you? For even sinners do the same. And if you lend to those from whom you hope to receive back, what credit is that to you? For even sinners lend to sinners to receive as much back. But love your enemies, do good, and lend, hoping for nothing in return; and your reward will be great, and you will be sons of the Most High. For He is kind to the unthankful and evil. Therefore, be merciful, just as your Father also is merciful. Judge not, and you shall not be judged. Condemn not, and you shall not be condemned. Forgive, and you will be forgiven.

— Luke 6:27-37

Bless those who persecute you; bless and do not curse...Beloved do not avenge yourselves, but rather give place to wrath; for it is written, "Vengeance is Mine, I will repay," says the Lord. Therefore "If your enemy is hungry, feed him; If he is thirsty, give him a drink; For in so doing you will heap coals of fire on his head. "Do not be overcome by evil but overcome evil with good.

—Romans 12:14, 19-21

NOTES:

Failure

- Failures and shortcomings are part of life.
- When we fail or fall, the Lord can lift us up if we call on Him.
- Believers should not rejoice at the fall or failure of others. Doing so displeases the Lord.
- When other individuals fail or fall, the believers should see it as an opportunity to show them God's love, compassion, mercy and grace.
- It is a good time to point them to the Lord—the only perfect One.
- Without the help of the Holy Spirit, anyone can fail/fall.

The Lord upholds all who fall and raises up all who are bowed down. The eyes of all look expectantly to You, And You give them their food in due season. You open Your hand and satisfy the desire of every living thing.

—Psalms 145:14–16

For a righteous man may fall seven times and rise again, But the wicked shall fall by calamity. Do not rejoice when your enemy falls, and do not let your heart be glad when he stumbles; Lest the Lord see it, and it displeases Him, And He turns away His wrath from him.

— Proverbs 24:16–18

Though the fig tree may not blossom, Nor fruit be on the vines; Though the labor of the olive may fail, And the fields yield no food; Though the flock may be cut off from the fold, And there be no herd in the stalls Yet I will rejoice in the Lord, I will joy in the God of my salvation.

—Habakkuk 3:17–18

NOTES:

Favor

- The Lord extravagantly and consistently shows His favor to those who seek Him, trust Him, and live according to His Word.
- Useful verses for encouraging believers to confidently maintain their trust in the Lord, even in times of personal hardship.
- A period of hardship in our lives is no evidence that God's favor or loving kindness has ceased.
- God's loving kindness toward His people will never cease!!

Thus, he left all that he had in Joseph's hand, and he did not know what he had except for the bread which he ate. Now Joseph was handsome in form and appearance...But the Lord was with Joseph and showed him mercy, and He gave him favor in the sight of the keeper of the prison.

–Genesis 39:6, 21

Wait on the Lord; Be of good courage, And He shall strengthen your heart; Wait, I say, on the Lord!

—Psalms 27:14

I love those who love me, and those who seek me diligently will find me. Riches and honor are with me, Enduring riches and righteousness.

—Proverbs 8:17–18

A good man obtains favor from the Lord, but a man of wicked intentions He will condemn.

—Proverbs 12:2

If anyone serves Me, him My Father will honor.

—John 12:26

NOTES:

Favoritism

- Useful verses for discouraging racism, sexism, tribalism, islamophobia, antisemitism, and vices such as these especially among believers.
- The Lord loves all people equally and wants them to come to the saving knowledge of Christ.
- The Lord is not a respecter of persons.
- All saved souls are equal before the Lord no matter their background.

Blessed is that man who makes the Lord his trust, and does not respect the proud, nor such as turn aside to lies.

—Psalms 40:4

Then Peter opened his mouth and said: "In truth I perceive that God shows no partiality.

—Acts 10:34

...where there is neither Greek nor Jew, circumcised nor uncircumcised, barbarian, Scythian, slave nor free, but Christ is all and in all...But he who does wrong will be repaid for what he has done, and there is no partiality.

—Colossians 3:11, 25

I charge you before God and the Lord Jesus Christ and the elect angels that you observe these things without prejudice, doing nothing with partiality.

—1 Timothy 5:21

But the wisdom that is from above is first pure, then peaceable, gentle, willing to yield, full of mercy and good fruits, without partiality and without hypocrisy.

—James 3:17

NOTES:

Finances

- Useful verses for reminding believers to pay their tithes and offerings to the Lord's house.
- The Lord always financially sustains those who do as He has commanded.
- The Lord knows our needs so we should depend on Him and not worry.
- For God's people, success, including financial success, results from obeying the word of God.
- Spiritual wealth is more important than financial wealth.

This Book of the Law shall not depart from your mouth, but you shall meditate in it day and night, that you may observe to do according to all that is written in it. For then you will make your way prosperous, and then you will have good success.

—Joshua 1:8

I love those who love me,
And those who seek me diligently will find me.
Riches and honor are with me,
Enduring riches and righteousness.
My fruit is better than gold, yes, than fine gold,
And my revenue than choice silver.

—Proverbs 8: 17-19

"Will a man rob God? Yet you have robbed Me! But you say, 'In what way have we robbed You?' In tithes and offerings. You are cursed with a curse, for you have robbed Me, Even this whole nation. Bring all the tithes into the storehouse, That there may be food in My house, And try Me now in this," Says the Lord of hosts, "If I will not open for you the windows of heaven And pour out for you such blessing That there will not be room enough to receive it."

—Malachi 3:8–10

Therefore, do not worry, saying, "What shall we eat?" or "What shall we drink?" or "What shall we wear?" For after all these things the Gentiles seek. For your heavenly Father knows that you need all these things. But seek first the kingdom of God and His righteousness, and all these things shall be added to you. Therefore, do not worry about tomorrow, for tomorrow will worry about its own things. Sufficient for the day is its own trouble.

—Matthew 6:31-34

Now as He was going out on the road, one came running, knelt before Him, and asked Him, "Good Teacher, what shall I do that I may inherit eternal life?" So Jesus said to him, "Why do you call Me good? No one is good but One, that is, God. You know the commandments: "Do not commit adultery, Do not murder, Do not steal, Do not bear false witness, Do not defraud, Honor your father and your mother. "And he answered and said to Him, "Teacher, all these things I have kept from my youth." Then Jesus, looking at him, loved him, and said to him, "One thing you lack: Go your way, sell whatever you have and give to the poor, and you will have treasure in heaven; and come, take up the cross, and follow Me." But he was sad at this word, and went away sorrowful, for he had great possessions. Then Jesus looked around and said to His disciples, "How hard it is for those who have riches to enter the kingdom of God!" And the disciples were astonished at His words. But Jesus answered again and said to them, "Children, how hard it is for those who trust in riches to enter the kingdom of God! It is easier for a camel to go through the eye of a needle than for a rich man to enter the kingdom of God." And they were greatly astonished, saying among themselves, "Who then can be saved?" But Jesus looked at them and said, "With men it is impossible, but not with God; for with God all things are possible." Then Peter began to say to Him, "See, we have left all and followed You." So Jesus answered and said, "Assuredly, I say to you, there is no one who has left house or brothers or sisters or father or mother or wife or children or lands, for My sake and the gospel's, who shall not receive a hundredfold now in this time—houses and brothers and sisters and mothers and children and lands, with persecutions—and in the age to come, eternal life. But many who are first will be last, and the last first."

—Mark 10:17–31

Give, and it will be given to you: good measure, pressed down, shaken together, and running over will be put into your bosom. For with the same measure that you use, it will be measured back to you.

—Luke 6:38

Come now, you who say, "Today or tomorrow we will go to such and such a city, spend a year there, buy and sell, and make a profit"; whereas you do not know what will happen tomorrow. For what is your life? It is even a vapor that appears for a little time and then vanishes away. Instead you ought to say, "If he Lord wills, we shall live and do this or that." But now you boast in your arrogance. All such boasting is evil. Therefore, to him who knows to do good and does not do it, to him it is sin.

—James 4:13–17

NOTES:

Forgiveness

- Believers are forgiven and saved so that they can demonstrate and illustrate to the people around us-the nature of God's love and forgiveness
- One reason our prayers are not answered is because we have refused to forgive others their sins against us.
- We always move into a superior spiritual position when we forgive others their sins against us.
- Asking God for forgiveness with an unforgiving heart (against others) is hypocritical and unacceptable to God.
- Believers must develop a forgiving attitude for the future because in the future, someone will wrong us.
- The Lord does not need your permission to forgive those who ask Him for forgiveness because of the wrong they did to you.

- It is the blood of His son that guarantees forgiveness for all and makes you forgivable when you sin against other people.
- Some people may deserve forgiveness because "they know not what they are doing" according to the Lord and Stephen.

He has not dealt with us according to our sins, nor punished us according to our iniquities. For as the heavens are high above the earth, so great is His mercy toward those who fear Him; As far as the east is from the west, so far has He removed our transgressions from us.

—Psalms 103:10-12

I, even I, am He who blots out your transgressions for My own sake; And I will not remember your sins.

—Isaiah 43:25

For if you forgive men their trespasses, your heavenly Father will also forgive you. But if you do not forgive men their trespasses, neither will your Father forgive your trespasses.

—Matthew 6:14–15

Then Peter came to Him and said, "Lord, how often shall my brother sin against me, and I forgive him? Up to seven times?"

Jesus said to him, "I do not say to you, up to seven times, but up to seventy times seven."

—Matthew 18:21–22

And whenever you stand praying, if you have anything against anyone, forgive him, that your Father in heaven may also forgive you your trespasses.

—Mark 11:25

And forgive us our sins, for we also forgive everyone who is indebted to us. And do not lead us into temptation. But deliver us from the evil one.

—Luke 11:4

And be kind to one another, tenderhearted, forgiving one another, just as God in Christ forgave you.

—Ephesians 4:32

...bearing with one another, and forgiving one another, if anyone has a complaint against another; even as Christ forgave you, so you also must do

—Colossians 3:13

If we confess our sins, He is faithful and just to forgive us our sins and to cleanse us from all unrighteousness.

—1 John 1:9

NOTES:

Freedom

- True spiritual freedom can only be found in Christ.
- There is no condemnation for those in Christ.
- A believer's spiritual freedom can become paralyzed by reckless loyalty to religion, denomination, or personalities instead to the Lord Himself.
- All human beings are fallible; therefore, a believer should keep looking unto Jesus the author and perfecter of our faith.

The Spirit of the Lord God is upon Me, Because the Lord has anointed Me To preach good tidings to the poor; He has sent Me to heal the brokenhearted, To proclaim liberty to the captives, And the opening of the prison to those who are bound
—Isaiah 61:1

Then Jesus said to those Jews who believed Him, "If you abide in My word, you are My disciples indeed. And you shall know the truth, and the truth shall make you free." They answered Him, "We are Abraham's descendants, and have never been in bondage to anyone. How can you say, 'You will be made free?'" Jesus answered them, "Most assuredly, I say to you, whoever commits sin is a slave of sin. And a slave does not abide in the house forever, but a son abides forever. Therefore, if the Son makes you free, you shall be free indeed.

—John 8:31–36

But now having been set free from sin, and having become slaves of God, you have your fruit to holiness, and the end, everlasting life.

—Romans 6:22

There is therefore now no condemnation to those who are in Christ Jesus, who do not walk according to the flesh, but according to the Spirit. For the law of the Spirit of life in Christ Jesus has made me free from the law of sin and death.

—Romans 8:1-2

Therefore let us also, seeing we are compassed about with so great a cloud of witnesses, lay aside every weight, and the sin which doth so easily beset us, and let us run with patience the race that is set before us, looking unto Jesus the author and perfecter of our faith, who for the joy that was set before him endured the cross, despising shame, and hath sat down at the right hand of the throne of God.

—Hebrew 12:1–2

NOTES:

Friendship

- Good friends are worth having and can be a blessing like Jonathan King David's friend.
- We must be careful and prayerful when choosing friends.
- We ought to make sure that our friends are godly.
- Parents should train and help their children to choose godly friends.

A friend loves at all times, and a brother is born for adversity.

—Proverbs 17:17

A man who has friends must himself be friendly, but there is a friend who sticks closer than a brother.

—Proverbs 18:24

No longer do I call you servants, for a servant does not know what his master is doing; but I have called you friends, for all things that I heard from My Father I have made known to you. You did not choose Me, but I chose you and appointed you that you should go and bear fruit, and that your fruit should remain, that whatever you ask the Father in My name He may give you.

These things I command you, that you love one another.

—John 15:15–17

Do not be deceived: "Evil company corrupts good habits."

—1 Corinthians 15:33

NOTES:

Gladness

- A close relationship with the Lord generates gladness no matter our situation.

Then he said to them, "Go your way, eat the fat, drink the sweet, and send portions to those for whom nothing is prepared; for this day is holy to our Lord. Do not sorrow, for the joy of the Lord is your strength." So the Levites quieted all the people, saying, "Be still, for the day is holy; do not be grieved."
—Nehemiah 8:10–11

O my God, my soul is cast down within me; Therefore, I will remember You from the land of the Jordan, And from the heights of Hermon, From the Hill Mizar.
—Psalms 42:6

Rejoice in the Lord always. Again, I will say, rejoice!
—Philippians 4:4

NOTES:

Gossip

- Gossiping is ungodly and evidence of spiritual immaturity.
- It displeases the Lord and is always a tool in the hands of the devil.
- Gossiping never leads to any good spiritual results.

You shall not go about as a talebearer among your people; nor shall you take a stand against the life of your neighbor: I am the Lord.

—Leviticus 19:16

Whoever secretly slanders his neighbor, Him I will destroy; The one who has a haughty look and a proud heart, Him I will not endure.

—Psalms 101:5

The words of a talebearer are like tasty trifles, and they go down into the inmost body. He who is slothful in his work Is a brother to him who is a great destroyer.

—Proverbs 18:8–9

For by your words you will be justified, and by your words you will be condemned.

—Matthew 12:37

Moreover, if your brother sins against you, go and tell him his fault between you and him alone. If he hears you, you have gained your brother.

—Matthew 18:15

Do not speak evil of one another, brethren. He who speaks evil of a brother and judges his brother, speaks evil of the law and judges the law. But if you judge the law, you are not a doer of the law but a judge. There is one Lawgiver, who is able to save and to destroy. Who are you to judge another?

—James 4:11–12

NOTES:

Gratitude (to God and Others)

- Showing gratitude to God publicly and continually, is part of being a believer.
- Believers show gratitude to God because of His works which no one else can match.
- Believers shout out gratitude to God because of who He is and His eternal goodness, love, faithfulness and mercy for His people.
- Gratitude and thanksgiving to God helps us count our blessing and see what we already have not what we want.
- Gratitude helps us build our godliness and contentment with what God has done for us.
- Gratitude to others is an extension of our gratitude to God.

- Gratitude to others helps us recognize godliness and Christian character in them.
- Gratitude to others encourages them to grow and mature in their Christian walk and works.
- Gratitude to God is a testimony to the world that we are not confused about the ultimate source of all our blessings.

Therefore I will give thanks to You, O LORD, among the Gentiles,
And sing praises to Your name

—2Samuel 22:50

Oh, give thanks to the LORD, for He is good! For His mercy endures forever.

—1Chronicles 16:34

And Hezekiah appointed the divisions of the priests and the Levites according to their divisions, each man according to his service, the priests and Levites for burnt offerings and peace offerings, to serve, to give thanks, and to praise in the gates of the camp of the LORD.

—2Chronicles 31:2

So Haman took the robe and the horse, arrayed Mordecai and led him on horseback through the city square, and proclaimed before him, 'Thus shall it be done to the man whom the king delights to honor!"

—Esther 6:11

Therefore I will give thanks to You, O LORD, among the Gentiles,
And sing praises to Your name.

—Psalm 18:49

Sing praise to the LORD, you saints of His,
And give thanks at the remembrance of His holy name. For His anger is but for a moment, His favor is for life; Weeping may endure for a night,
But joy comes in the morning.

—Psalm: 30:4-5

It is good to give thanks to the LORD,
And to sing praises to Your name, O Most High; To declare Your lovingkindness in the morning, And Your faithfulness every night

—Psalm 90:1-2

Oh, give thanks to the LORD, for He is good! For His mercy endures forever.

Let Israel now say, His mercy endures forever." Let the house of Aaron now say, "His mercy endures forever." Let those who fear the LORD now say, "His mercy endures forever."

—Psalm 118:1-4

So when this was done, the rest of those on the island who had diseases also came and were healed. They also honored us in many ways; and when we departed, they provided such things as were necessary.

—Acts 28:10

Render therefore to all their due: taxes to whom taxes are due, customs to whom customs, fear to whom fear, honor to whom honor.

—Romans 13:7

I commend to you Phoebe our sister, who is a servant of the church in Cenchrea, that you may receive her in the Lord in a manner worthy of the saints, and assist her in whatever business she has need of you; for indeed she has been a helper of many and of myself also.

—Romans 16:1-4

Therefore I also, after I heard of your faith in the Lord Jesus and your love for all the saints, do not cease to give thanks for you, making mention of you in my prayers: that the God of our Lord Jesus Christ, the Father of glory, may give to you the spirit of wisdom and revelation in the knowledge of Him,

—Ephesians 1:16-17

Let the elders who rule well be counted worthy of double honor, especially those who labor in the word and doctrine. For the Scripture says, "You shall not muzzle an ox while it treads out the grain," and, "The laborer is worthy of his wages."

—1 Timothy 5:17-18

NOTES:

Grief

- Useful verses for comforting those going through earthly pain, suffering and all sorts of grief.
- The Lord is never far from his people in times of grief.
- He ultimately will bring us His comfort if we continue to wait, trust, and lean on Him.
- He quickly arrived to comfort Mary and Martha after Lazarus died.

Surely, he took up our pain and bore our suffering, yet we considered him punished by God, stricken by him, and afflicted. But he was pierced for our transgressions, he was crushed for our iniquities; the punishment that brought us peace was on him, and by his wounds we are healed. We all, like sheep, have gone astray, each of us has turned to our own way; and the Lord has laid on him the iniquity of us all.

—Isaiah 53:4–6

The Lord is close to the brokenhearted and saves those who are crushed in spirit.

—Psalm 34:18

My flesh and my heart may fail, but God is the strength of my heart and my portion forever.

—Psalm 73:26

He heals the brokenhearted and binds up their wounds.

—Psalm 147:3

Blessed are those who mourn, for they will be comforted.

—Matthew 5:4

He will wipe every tear from their eyes. There will be no more death or mourning or crying or pain, for the old order of things has passed away.

—Revelation 21:4

NOTES:

Guilt

- Useful verses for encouraging people to confess their sins to the Lord and ask for forgiveness from Him.

Against You, you only, have I sinned, and done this evil in Your sight— That You may be found just when You speak, and blameless when You judge.

—Psalms 51:4

For all have sinned and fall short of the glory of God

—Romans 3:23

And having been set free from sin, you became slaves of righteousness.

—Romans 6:18

Therefore, if anyone is in Christ, he is a new creation; old things have passed away; behold, all things have become new.

—2 Corinthians 5:17

In Him we have redemption through His blood, the forgiveness of sins, according to the riches of His grace

—Ephesians 1:7

For by grace you have been saved through faith, and that not of yourselves; it is the gift of God, not of works, lest anyone should boast.

—Ephesians 2:8-9

If we confess our sins, He is faithful and just to forgive us our sins and to cleanse us from all unrighteousness.

—1 John 1:9

NOTES:

Healing

- The Lord is still a healer.
- Ultimate healing comes from the hand of the Lord.
- Physical healing is not as important as spiritual healing and reconciliation to God.
- God can glorify Himself through sickness in our body.

Surely, He has borne our griefs, and carried our sorrows; Yet we esteemed Him stricken, Smitten by God, and afflicted. But He was wounded for our transgressions, He was bruised for our iniquities; The chastisement for our peace was upon Him, And by His stripes we are healed.

—Isaiah 53:4–5

Again, I say to you that if two of you agree on earth concerning anything that they ask, it will be done for them by My Father in heaven.

—Matthew 18:19

When the sun was setting, all those who had any that were sick with various diseases brought them to Him; and He laid His hands on every one of them and healed them.

—Luke 4:40

Then Jesus said to those Jews who believed Him, "If you abide in My word, you are My disciples indeed. And you shall know the truth, and the truth shall make you free."

—John 8:31–32

So then faith comes by hearing, and hearing by the word of God.

—Romans 10:17

And lest I should be exalted above measure by the abundance of the revelations, a thorn in the flesh was given to me, a messenger of Satan to buffet me, lest I be exalted above measure. Concerning this thing I pleaded with the Lord three times that it might depart from me. And He said to me, "My grace is sufficient for you, for My strength is made perfect in weakness." Therefore, most gladly I will rather boast in my infirmities, that the power of Christ may rest upon me. Therefore, I take pleasure in infirmities, in reproaches, in needs, in persecutions, in distresses, for Christ's sake. For when I am weak, then I am strong.

—2 Corinthians 12:7–10

Is any sick among you? let him call for the elders of the church; and let them pray over him, anointing him with oil in the name of the Lord: And the prayer of faith shall save the sick, and the Lord shall raise him up; and if he has committed sins, they shall be forgiven him.

—James 5:14–15

NOTES:

His Word

- The words and decrees of the Lord will never fail; they will always come true as He said.
- God is under no obligation to fulfill a misinterpretation of His word.
- Misinterpretations of God's Word (intentional or negligent) do not have the guarantee of His faithfulness.
- If it is truly God's promise and word, it will definitely come to pass.

And God said, "Let there be light" and there was light... Then God said, "Let the waters under the heavens be gathered together into one place, and let the dry land appear"; and it was so...Then God said, "Let the earth bring forth grass, the herb that yields seed, and the fruit tree that yields fruit according to its kind, whose seed is in itself, on the earth" and it was

*so...and let them be for lights in the firmament of the heavens
to give light on the earth"; and it was so.*

—Genesis 1:3,9,11,15

*So the Lord has fulfilled His word which He spoke, and
I have filled the position of my father David, and sit on the
throne of Israel, as the Lord promised; and I have built the
temple for the name of the Lord God of Israel.*

—2 Chronicles 6:10

*And now, behold, the Lord has kept me alive, as He said,
these forty-five years, ever since the Lord spoke this word to
Moses while Israel wandered in the wilderness; and now, here
I am this day, eighty-five years old.*

—Joshua 14:10

*"Behold, this day I am going the way of all the earth. And
you know in all your hearts and in all your souls that not one
thing has failed of all the good things which the LORD your
God spoke concerning you. All have come to pass for you; not
one word of them has failed."*

—Joshua 23:14

*Let them praise the name of the Lord, For He commanded,
and they were created. He also established them forever and
ever; He made a decree which shall not pass away. Praise the*

Lord from the earth, you great sea creatures and all the depths; Fire and hail, snow and clouds; Stormy wind, fulfilling His word.

—Psalms 148:5–8

So shall My word be that goes forth from My mouth; It shall not return to Me void, but it shall accomplish what I please, and it shall prosper in the thing for which I sent it.

—Isaiah 55:11

Heaven and earth will pass away, but My words will by no means pass away.

—Matthew 24:35

Heaven and earth will pass away, but My words will by no means pass away.

—Mark 13:31

When He had said this, He went on ahead, going up to Jerusalem. And it came to pass, when He drew near to Bethphage and Bethany, at the mountain called Olivet, that He sent two of His disciples, saying, "Go into the village opposite you, whereas you enter you will find a colt tied, on which no one has ever sat. Loose it and bring it here. And if anyone asks you, 'Why are you losing it?' thus you shall say to him, 'Because the Lord has need of it.'" So those who were sent went their way and found it just as He had said to them. But as they were losing the colt, the owners of it said to them, "Why are you losing the colt?"

—Luke 19:28–33

Heaven and earth will pass away, but My words will by no means pass away.

—Luke 21:33

Then came the day of Unleavened Bread on which the Passover lamb had to be sacrificed. Jesus sent Peter and John, saying, "Go and make preparations for us to eat the Passover." "Where do you want us to prepare for it?" they asked. He replied, "As you enter the city, a man carrying a jar of water will meet you. Follow him to the house that he enters, and say to the owner of the house, 'The Teacher asks: Where is the guest room, where I may eat the Passover with my disciples?' He will show you a large room upstairs, all furnished. Make preparations there." They left and found things just as Jesus had told them. So they prepared the Passover.

—Luke 22:7–13 (NIV)

But the word of the Lord endures forever. Now this is the word which by the gospel was preached to you.

—1 Peter 1:25

NOTES:

Homosexuality

- Useful verses for spiritual education on what the Bible teaches about homosexuality.
- Useful, not for judgment and condemnation, but for encouraging repentance as is the case with all other sexual sins (see "Sexual Sins").

You shall not lie with a male as with a woman. It is an abomination.

— Leviticus 18:22

If a man lies with a male as he lies with a woman, both of them have committed an abomination. They shall surely be put to death. Their blood shall be upon them.

—Leviticus 20:13

Because, although they knew God, they did not glorify Him as God, nor were thankful, but became futile in their thoughts, and their foolish hearts were darkened.

—Romans 1:21

For this reason, God gave them up to vile passions. For even their women exchanged the natural use for what is against nature. Likewise, also the men, leaving the natural use of the woman, burned in their lust for one another, men with men committing what is shameful, and receiving in themselves the penalty of their error which was due.

—Romans 1:26–27

Likewise, you also, reckon yourselves to be dead indeed to sin, but alive to God in Christ Jesus our Lord. Therefore, do not let sin reign in your mortal body, that you should obey it in its lusts. And do not present your members as instruments of unrighteousness to sin but present yourselves to God as being alive from the dead, and your members as instruments of righteousness to God. For sin shall not have dominion over you, for you are not under law but under grace.

—Romans 6:11–14

But know this, that in the last days perilous times will come: For men will be lovers of themselves, lovers of money, boasters, proud, blasphemers, disobedient to parents, un-

thankful, unholy, unloving, unforgiving, slanderers, without self-control, brutal, despisers of good, traitors, headstrong, haughty, lovers of pleasure rather than lovers of God,

—2 Timothy 3:1–4

NOTES:

Hope

- The hope of believers, at all times and in all situations, should be in the Lord.
- The believer's hope should be placed on "nothing else but Jesus' blood and righteousness."

...through whom also we have access by faith into this grace in which we stand and rejoice in hope of the glory of God.
—Romans 5:2

...bears all things, believes all things, hopes all things, endures all things.
—1 Corinthians 13:7

To them God willed to make known what the riches of the glory of this mystery among the Gentiles are: which is Christ in you, the hope of glory.
—Colossians 1:27

NOTES:

Humility

- A spiritually important character required by God of all God's servants and people.
- An attitude that recognizes that all we are and have is made possible by the Lord.
- All those God himself called His servants in the Bible, had this character and attitude.

Before destruction the heart of a man is haughty (proud),
And before honor is humility.

—Proverbs 18:12

So the last will be first, and the first last. For many are called, but few chosen.

—Matthew 20:16

For even the Son of Man did not come to be served, but to serve, and to give His life a ransom for many.

—Mark 10:45

Let this mind be in you, which was also in Christ Jesus, who, being in the form of God, did not consider it robbery to be equal with God, but made Himself of no reputation, taking the form of a bondservant, and coming in the likeness of men. And being found in appearance as a man, He humbled Himself and became obedient to the point of death, even the death of the cross. Therefore, God also has highly exalted Him and given Him the name, which is above every name, that at the name of Jesus every knee should bow, of those in heaven, and of those on earth, and of those under the earth, and that every tongue should confess that Jesus Christ is Lord, to the glory of God the Father.

—Philippians 2:5–11

But He gives more grace. Therefore, He says: "God resists the proud, but gives grace to the humble." Humble yourselves in the sight of the Lord, and He will lift you up.

—James 4:6, 10

NOTES:

EMMANUEL AHIA

Injustice

- Every human being will suffer a form of injustice here on earth because it is always a tool in the hands of the devil.
- All God's people can be sure that the Lord will ultimately give them justice because that is His promise.
- God can use unjust situations to lift up His people, to align His people to His will, and to bring glory to His name.
- God's power is always greater than human injustice.
- Violence is not a biblically defensible response to injustice.
- The Apostle Peter did not need to cut off anyone's ear just because he was witnessing injustice.
- Our God is a just God.

When the Lord saw that Leah was unloved, He opened her womb; but Rachel was barren.

—Genesis 29:31

You shall do no injustice in judgment. You shall not be partial to the poor, nor honor the person of the mighty. In righteousness you shall judge your neighbor. You shall not go about as a talebearer among your people; nor shall you take a stand against the life of your neighbor: I am the LORD.

— Leviticus 19:15

Vengeance is Mine, and recompense; Their foot shall slip in due time; For the day of their calamity is at hand, And the things to come hasten upon them.

—Deuteronomy 32:35

Does God subvert judgment? Or does the Almighty pervert justice?

—Job 8:3

My face is flushed from weeping, and on my eyelids is the shadow of death; Although no violence is in my hands,
And my prayer is pure.

—Job 16:16–17

God stands in the congregation of the mighty; He judges among the gods. How long will you judge unjustly, and show partiality to the wicked? Selah Defend the poor and fatherless; Do justice to the afflicted and needy.

—Psalms 82:1–3

You have a mighty arm; Strong is Your hand, and high is Your right hand. Righteousness and justice are the foundation of Your throne; Mercy and truth go before Your face.

—Psalms 89:13-14

He who oppresses the poor reproaches his Maker, but he who honors Him has mercy on the needy. The wicked is banished in his wickedness, But the righteous has a refuge in his death.

— Proverbs 14:31

An unjust man is an abomination to the righteous, and he who is upright in the way is an abomination to the wicked.

—Proverbs 29:27

Tell and bring forth your case; Yes, let them take counsel together. Who has declared this from ancient time? Who has told it from that time? Have not I, the Lord? And there is no other God besides Me, A just God and a Savior; There is none besides Me.

—Isaiah 45:21

Then Simon Peter, having a sword, drew it and struck the high priest's servant, and cut off his right ear. The servant's name was Malchus. So Jesus said to Peter, "Put your sword into the sheath. Shall I not drink the cup which My Father has given Me?"

—John 18:10-11

Beloved, do not avenge yourselves, but rather give place to wrath; for it is written, "Vengeance is Mine, I will repay," says the Lord.

—Romans 12:19

NOTES:

Joy

- The joy of a believer comes from our relationship with and hope in the Lord.
- It should not depend on our circumstances.
- The joy of the Lord should be the believers' strength.

Then he said to them, "Go your way, eat the fat, drink the sweet, and send portions to those for whom nothing is prepared; for this day is holy to our Lord. Do not sorrow, for the joy of the LORD is your strength."
—Nehemiah 8:10

You will show me the path of life; In Your presence is fullness of joy; At Your right hand are pleasures forevermore.
—Psalms 16:11

Praise the Lord! Blessed is the man who fears the Lord, who delights greatly in His commandments.

—Psalms 112:1

For I delight in the law of God according to the inward man.

—Romans 7:22

Rejoice in the Lord always. Again, I will say, rejoice!

—Philippians 4:4

NOTES:

Judgment

- God's judgment is just and will be the ultimate and final.
- Human judgment is usually imperfect and may be partial and selfish.
- No one will escape God's final judgment.

For with what judgment you judge, you will be judged; and with the measure you use, it will be measured back to you. And why do you look at the speck in your brother's eye, but do not consider the plank in your own eye? Or how can you say to your brother, 'Let me remove the speck from your eye'; and look, a plank is in your own eye? Hypocrite! First remove the plank from your own eye, and then you will see clearly to remove the speck from your brother's eye.

— Matthew 7:2–5

Judge not, and you shall not be judged. Condemn not, and you shall not be condemned. Forgive, and you will be forgiven.

—Luke 6:37

Then I saw a great white throne and Him who sat on it, from whose face the earth and the heaven fled away. And there was found no place for them.And I saw the dead, small and great, standing before God, and books were opened. And another book was opened, which is the Book of Life. And the dead were judged according to their works, by the things which were written in the books. The sea gave up the dead who were in it, and Death and Hades delivered up the dead who were in them. And they were judged, each one according to his works. Then Death and Hades were cast into the lake of fire. This is the second death. And anyone not found written in the Book of Life was cast into the lake of fire.

—Revelation 20:11–15

NOTES:

Laziness

- Laziness usually leads to poverty. It is inconsistent with godliness.
- Lazy pastors or bible teachers may be unable to "rightly divide" the word of truth.

Go to the ant, you sluggard! Consider her ways and be wise,

—Proverbs 6:6

He who has a slack hand becomes poor, But the hand of the diligent makes rich. He who gathers in summer is a wise son; He who sleeps in harvest is a son who causes shame.

—Proverbs 10:4–5

The hand of the diligent will rule, but the lazy man will be put to forced labor.

—Proverbs 12:24

Study to shew thyself approved unto God, a workman that needs not to be ashamed, rightly dividing the word of truth.
—2 Timothy 2:15

NOTES:

Lies/False Witness

- The devil is the chief liar.
- All lies are contrary to God's character and will be judged by God.
- It is God's requirement that the believer should always support and stand for the truth.

You shall not bear false witness against your neighbor.
—Exodus 20:16

A worthless person, a wicked man, walks with a perverse mouth; He winks with his eyes, he shuffles his feet, he points with his fingers; Perversity is in his heart, he devises evil continually, he sows discord. Therefore, his calamity shall come suddenly; Suddenly he shall be broken without remedy. These six things the Lord hates, yes, seven are an abomination to Him: A proud look, a lying tongue, hands that shed innocent blood, A heart that devises wicked plans, Feet that are swift in running to evil, A false witness who speaks lies, and one who sows discord among brethren.

—Proverbs 6:12-19

A false witness will not go unpunished, and he who speaks lies will not escape. Many entreat the favor of the nobility, and every man is a friend to one who gives gifts. All the brothers of the poor hate him; How much more do his friends go far from him! He may pursue them with words, yet they abandon him. He who gets wisdom loves his own soul; He who keeps understanding will find good. A false witness will not go unpunished, and he who speaks lies shall perish.

—Proverbs 19:5–9

NOTES:

Loneliness

- God's people who are in intimate relationship with Him are never truly alone.
- Loneliness is usually experienced in ungodly relationships.
- Drawing closer to God, and God's people, is the answer to existential loneliness (see "Abandonment").

And the Lord, He is the one who goes before you. He will be with you; He will not leave you nor forsake you; do not fear nor be dismayed.

—Deuteronomy 31:8

Yea, though I walk through the valley of the shadow of death, I will fear no evil; For You are with me; Your rod and Your staff, they comfort me

—Psalms 23:4

I will not leave you orphans; I will come to you.

—John 14:18

NOTES:

EMMANUEL AHIA

Love

- To truly experience love, we must first love the Lord.
- If we truly love the Lord, we will become able to truly love others.
- Lust is not love.

Jesus said to him, "You shall love the Lord your God with all your heart, with all your soul, and with all your mind." This is the first and great commandment.

—Matthew 22:37

A new commandment I give to you, that you love one another; as I have loved you, that you also love one another. By this all will know that you are My disciples, if you have love for one another.

—John 13:34-35

Love suffers long and is kind; love does not envy; love does not parade itself, is not puffed up; does not behave rudely, does not seek its own, is not provoked, thinks no evil; does not rejoice in iniquity, but rejoices in the truth; bears all things, believes all things, hopes all things, endures all things. Love never fails. But whether there are prophecies, they will fail; whether there are tongues, they will cease; whether there is knowledge, it will vanish away.

—1 Corinthians 13:4-8

But the fruit of the Spirit is love, joy, peace, longsuffering, kindness, goodness, faithfulness, gentleness, self-control. Against such there is no law.

—Galatians 5:22–23

and from Jesus Christ, the faithful witness, the firstborn from the dead, and the ruler over the kings of the earth. To Him who loved us and washed us from our sins in His own blood,

—Revelation 1:5

NOTES:

Lust

- Lust is not love. It arises out of human fleshly desires and sinful nature.
- It is toxic to godliness, righteousness, and healthy Christian character.
- It is also one of the tools the devil uses to destroy God's people.
- Believers should flee from all forms of lust.

Now Samson went to Gaza and saw a harlot there, and went in to her. When the Gazites were told, "Samson has come here," they surrounded the place and lay in wait for him all night at the gate of the city. They were quiet all night, saying, "In the morning, when it is daylight, we will kill him."

—Judges 16:1-2

Therefore, do not let sin reign in your mortal body, that you should obey it in its lusts.

—Romans 6:12

Now the works of the flesh are evident, which are: adultery, fornication, uncleanness, lewdness, idolatry, sorcery, hatred, contentions, jealousies, outbursts of wrath, selfish ambitions, dissensions, heresies, envy, murders, drunkenness, revelries, and the like; of which I tell you beforehand, just as I also told you in time past, that those who practice such things will not inherit the kingdom of God.

—Galatians 5:19–21

Flee also youthful lusts; but pursue righteousness, faith, love, peace with those who call on the Lord out of a pure heart. But avoid foolish and ignorant disputes, knowing that they generate strife.

—2 Timothy 2:22

For all that is in the world--the lust of the flesh, the lust of the eyes, and the pride of life--is not of the Father but is of the world.

—1 John 2:16

NOTES:

Marriage

- Marriage was established by God for physical, social, psychological, and spiritual intimacy between a man and a woman.
- He intended it to last a lifetime (see Divorce).
- Marriage should be based on love, not lust.
- Unmarried Christians should seek the will of God concerning marriage.

And the Lord God said, "It is not good that man should be alone; I will make him a helper comparable to him."
—Genesis 2:18

He who finds a wife finds a good thing and obtains favor from the Lord.
—Proverbs 18:22

Live joyfully with the wife whom you love all the days of your vain life which He has given you under the sun, all your days of vanity; for that is your portion in life, and in the labor which you perform under the sun.

—Ecclesiastes 9:9

And He looked around to see her who had done this thing.

—Matthew 5:32

The Pharisees also came to Him, testing Him, and saying to Him, "Is it lawful for a man to divorce his wife for just any reason?" And He answered and said to them, "Have you not read that He who made them at the beginning 'made them male and female,' and said, 'For this reason a man shall leave his father and mother and be joined to his wife, and the two shall become one flesh'? So then, they are no longer two but one flesh. Therefore, what God has joined together, let not man separate." They said to Him, "Why then did Moses command to give a certificate of divorce, and to put her away?" He said to them, "Moses, because of the hardness of your hearts, permitted you to divorce your wives, but from the beginning it was not so."

—Matthew 19:3–8

Therefore, what God has joined together, let not man separate.

—Mark 10:9

...but if they cannot exercise self-control, let them marry. For it is better to marry than to burn with passion. Now to the married I command, yet not I but the Lord: A wife is not to depart from her husband. But even if she does depart, let her remain unmarried or be reconciled to her husband. And a husband is not to divorce his wife.

—1 Corinthians 7:9–11

Likewise, their wives must be reverent, not slanderers, temperate, faithful in all things.

—1 Timothy 3:11

Therefore, I desire that the younger widows marry, bear children, manage the house, give no opportunity to the adversary to speak reproachfully.

—1 Timothy 5:14

Marriage is honorable among all, and the bed undefiled; but fornicators and adulterers God will judge...

Therefore, by Him let us continually offer the sacrifice of praise to God, that is, the fruit of our lips, giving thanks to His name.

—Hebrews 13:4,15

NOTES:

Mental Health

- Close relationship with the Lord promotes healthy mental health – peace, contentment, forgiveness, patience, hope, etc.
- There are forms of mental dysfunction for which a believer should consult a psychiatrist or other mental health professionals.
- It is not sinful for a believer to use medication to help with serious mental illness.

Blessed is the man Who walks not in the counsel of the ungodly, nor stands in the path of sinners, nor sits in the seat of the scornful; But his delight is in the law of the Lord, and in His law, he meditates day and night.

He shall be like a tree Planted by the rivers of water, that brings forth its fruit in its season, whose leaf also shall not wither; and whatever he does shall prosper.

—Psalms 1:1–3

You will keep him in perfect peace, whose mind is stayed on You, because he trusts in You.

—Isaiah 26:3

And do not be conformed to this world, but be transformed by the renewing of your mind, that you may prove what is that good and acceptable and perfect will of God.

—Romans 12:2

Finally, brethren, whatever things are true, whatever things are noble, whatever things are just, whatever things are pure, whatever things are lovely, whatever things are of good report, if there is any virtue and if there is anything praiseworthy--meditate on these things.

—Philippians 4:8

NOTES:

Obedience/ Disobedience

- Disobedience of God's word usually leads to tragic consequences.
- The Lord is always pleased with those who obey His word and will.

Thus Noah did according to all that God commanded him, so he did.

—Genesis 6:22

So Samuel said: "Has the Lord as great delight in burnt offerings and sacrifices, as in obeying the voice of the Lord? Behold, to obey is better than sacrifice, and to heed than the fat of rams."

—1 Samuel 15:22

I have restrained my feet from every evil way, That I may keep Your word.

—Psalms 119:101

"If you love Me, keep My commandments."

—John 14:15

NOTES:

Parent/Child

- Godly parents should bring up their children in the Lord and for the Lord.
- Abraham was instructed by the Lord to do so.

Observe and obey all these words which I command you, that it may go well with you and your children after you forever, when you do what is good and right in the sight of the Lord your God.

—Deuteronomy 12:28

He who spares his rod hates his son, but he who loves him disciplines him promptly.

—Proverbs 13:24

Train up a child in the way he should go, and when he is old, he will not depart from it.

—Proverbs 22:6

The rod and rebuke give wisdom, but a child left to himself brings shame to his mother.

—Proverbs 29:15

Children obey your parents in the Lord, for this is right. "Honor your father and mother," which is the first commandment with promise: "that it may be well with you and you may live long on the earth."

—Ephesians 6:1–3

For whom the Lord loves He chastens and scourges every son whom He receives. If you endure chastening, God deals with you as with sons; for what son is there whom a father does not chasten?

—Hebrews 12:6–7

For they indeed for a few days chastened us as seemed best to them, but He for our profit, that we may be partakers of His holiness. Now no chastening seems to be joyful for the present, but painful; nevertheless, afterward it yields the peaceable fruit of righteousness to those who have been trained by it.

—Hebrews 12:10–11

NOTES:

Parenting

- Begin early to raise children in the ways of the Lord.
- Lead your children to the Lord.
- Remain diligent, consistent and faithful. Do not be half hazard.
- Remain prayerful as Job was.
- Be loving, positive and patient even when you discipline and correct a child.
- Teach what should be done not only what should not be done.
- Throughout the time of the Priest Jehoiada, Joash did what was right in the LORD's sight because he was spiritually dependent on Jehoiada.
- Teach children to have personal and direct relationship with the Lord not just depend on you. The Lord Himself will give them the best spiritual direction and stability for life.
- Give biblical reasons why things should or should not be done.

- Remain an example and admit your shortcomings.
- Teach forgiveness and practice it with your children.
- Be flexible when the Word is not compromised, and a child's personality calls for it.
- Bless your children. Do not curse them.
- Ask the Lord for wisdom and continue to depend on Him when things get rough.
- Today's Godly parenting will become a good foundation for the next generation.

For I have chosen him so that he will (raise) command his children and his house after him to keep the way of the LORD by doing what is right and just. This is how the LORD will fulfill to Abraham what he promised him.

—Genesis 18:19

Then his father Isaac said to him, "Please come closer and kiss me, my son."

So he came closer and kissed him. When Isaac smelled his clothes, he blessed him and said:

—Genesis 27:27

Only be on your guard and diligently watch yourselves, so that you don't forget the things your eyes have seen and so that they don't slip from your mind as long as you live. Teach them to your children and your grandchildren.

—Deuteronomy 4:9

These words that I am giving you today are to be in your heart. Repeat them to your children. Talk about them when you sit in your house and when you walk along the road, when you lie down and when you get up. Bind them as a sign on your hand and let them be a symbol on your forehead. Write them on the doorposts of your house and on your city gates.

—Deuteronomy 6: 6-9

However, after Jehoiada died, the rulers of Judah came and paid homage to the king. Then the king listened to them, and they abandoned the temple of the LORD, the God of their ancestors, and served the Asherah poles and the idols. So there was wrath against Judah and Jerusalem for this guilt of theirs.

—2 Chronicles 24:2 &17

His sons used to take turns having banquets at their homes. They would send an invitation to their three sisters to eat and drink with them. Whenever a round of banqueting was over, Job would send for his children and purify them, rising early in the morning to offer burnt offerings for all of them. For Job thought, "Perhaps my children have sinned, having cursed God in their hearts." This was Job's regular practice.

—Job 1:4-5

I have treasured your word in my heart
so that I may not sin against you—Your word is a lamp for
my feet and a light on my path.

—Psalm 119: 11 & 109

Listen, my son, to your father's instruction,
and don't reject your mother's teaching,

—Proverbs 1:8

Trust in the LORD with all your heart,
and do not rely on your own understanding;
in all your ways know him,
and he will make your paths straight.
Don't be wise in your own eyes;
fear the LORD and turn away from evil.

—Proverbs 3:5-7

The one who will not use the rod hates his son, but the one
who loves him disciplines him diligently.

—Proverbs 13:24

Discipline your son while there is hope;
don't set your heart on being the cause of his death.

—Proverbs 19:18

Train up a child in the way he should go,
And even when he is old, he will not depart from it.
Foolishness is bound up in the heart of a child; But the rod
of correction shall drive it far from him.

—Proverbs 22:6,22

Let a man so account of us, as of ministers of Christ, and
stewards of the mysteries of God. Here, moreover, it is re-
quired in stewards, that a man be found faithful.

—1 Corinthians 4:1- 2

Love is patient, love is kind. Love does not envy, is not
boastful, is not arrogant, is not rude, is not self-seeking, is not
irritable, and does not keep a record of wrongs. Love finds no
joy in unrighteousness but rejoices in the truth. It bears all
things, believes all things, hopes all things, endures all things.
Love never ends.

—1 Corinthians 13:4–7

Let all bitterness, and wrath, and anger, and clamor, and
railing, be put away from you, with all malice: and be ye kind
one to another, tenderhearted, forgiving each other, even as
God also in Christ forgave you.

—Ephesians 4: 31–32

And, ye fathers, provoke not your children to wrath: but nurture them in the chastening and admonition of the Lord.

—Ephesians 6:4

pray without ceasing; in everything give thanks: for this is the will of God in Christ Jesus to you-ward.

—1 Thessalonians 5:17-18

All Scripture is inspired by God and is profitable for teaching, for rebuking, for correcting, for training in righteousness, so that the man of God may be complete, equipped for every good work.

—2 Timothy 3:16-17

NOTES:

Peace

- The peace of God is available to those who love and trust Him.
- The peace from God is administered by the Holy Spirit and transcends human understanding.

Peace I leave with you, my peace I give to you; not as the world gives do I give to you. Let not your heart be troubled, neither let it be afraid.

—John 14:27

Be anxious for nothing, but in everything by prayer and supplication, with thanksgiving, let your requests be made known to God; and the peace of God, which surpasses all understanding, will guard your hearts and minds through Christ Jesus.

—Philippians 4:6–7

And let the peace of God rule in your hearts, to which also you were called in one body: and be thankful.

—Colossians 3:15

NOTES:

Praise

- Useful verses to assure every Christian that no matter our situation or issues, we must continue to praise and worship the Lord.
- It is a way of life for Spirit-filled believers.
- It is always the devil's wish that we stop praising the Lord especially when we are facing difficult life situations.

Therefore the Lord God of Israel says: "I said indeed that your house and the house of your father would walk before Me forever." But now the Lord says: "Far be it from Me; for those who honor Me, I will honor, and those who despise Me shall be lightly esteemed."

—1 Samuel 2:30

But You are holy, Enthroned in the praises of Israel.

—Psalms 22:3

Whoever offers praise glorifies Me; And to him who orders his conduct aright I will show the salvation of God."
—Psalms 50:23

It is good to give thanks to the Lord, and to sing praises to Your name, O Most High; to declare Your lovingkindness in the morning, And Your faithfulness every night,
—Psalms 92:1-2

Oh come, let us worship and bow down; Let us kneel before the Lord our Maker.
—Psalms 95:6

For this reason, I bow my knees to the Father of our Lord Jesus Christ,
—Ephesians 3:14

...speaking to one another in psalms and hymns and spiritual songs, singing and making melody in your heart to the Lord,
—Ephesians 5:19

...in everything give thanks; for this is the will of God in Christ Jesus for you.
—1 Thessalonians 5:18

Therefore, by Him let us continually offer the sacrifice of praise to God, that is, the fruit of our lips, giving thanks to His name.

—Hebrews 13:15

NOTES:

Prayer

- Believers serve a prayer answering God.
- His answers to our prayers are not usually what we want, but always what we need.
- His answer may be yes, no, or wait.
- Delay in seeing any answer to our prayer does not mean that He has not heard us.

And she was in bitterness of soul and prayed to the Lord and wept in anguish.

For this child I prayed, and the Lord has granted me my petition which I asked of Him.

—1 Samuel. 1:10, 27

He went in therefore, shut the door behind the two of them, and prayed to the Lord.

—2 Kings 4:33

Return and tell Hezekiah the leader of My people, 'Thus says the Lord, the God of David your father: "I have heard your prayer, I have seen your tears; surely, I will heal you. On the third day you shall go up to the house of the Lord."

—2 Kings 20:5

If My people who are called by My name will humble themselves, and pray and seek My face, and turn from their wicked ways, then I will hear from heaven, and will forgive their sin and heal their land.

—2 Chronicles 7:14

So it was, when I heard these words, that I sat down and wept, and mourned for many days; I was fasting and praying before the God of heaven.

—Nehemiah 1:4

And the Lord restored Job's losses when he prayed for his friends. Indeed, the Lord gave Job twice as much as he had before.

—Job 42:10

He shall regard the prayer of the destitute and shall not despise their prayer.

—Psalms 102:17

The sacrifice of the wicked is an abomination to the LORD, But the prayer of the upright is His delight.

—Proverbs 15:8

The Lord is far from the wicked, But He hears the prayer of the righteous.

—Proverbs 15:29

And I prayed to the Lord my God, and made confession, and said, "O Lord, great and awesome God, who keeps His covenant and mercy with those who love Him, and with those who keep His commandments

—Daniel 9:4

Again, I say to you that if two of you agree on earth concerning anything that they ask, it will be done for them by My Father in heaven.

—Matthew 18:19

And whatever things you ask in prayer, believing, you will receive.

—Matthew 21:22

Then He spoke a parable to them, that men always ought to pray and not lose heart,

—Luke 18:1

If you abide in Me, and My words abide in you, you will ask what you desire, and it shall be done for you.

—John 15:7

...praying always with all prayer and supplication in the Spirit, being watchful to this end with all perseverance and supplication for all the saints

—Ephesians 6:18

Be anxious for nothing, but in everything by prayer and supplication, with thanksgiving, let your requests be made known to God.

—Philippians 4:6

pray without ceasing

—1 Thessalonians 5:17

For the eyes of the Lord are on the righteous, And His ears are open to their prayers; But the face of the Lord is against those who do evil."

—1 Peter 3:12

NOTES:

Pride

- Pride is a manifest tool in the hand of the devil. That was, in fact, why he was thrown out of heaven.
- Proud people typically do not acknowledge God in anything they do, say, or achieve.
- Pride is a product of the flesh.
- God answers the prayers of the humble (see "Humility")

But when he was strong his heart was lifted up, to his destruction, for he transgressed against the Lord his God by entering the temple of the Lord to burn incense on the altar of incense. So Azariah the priest went in after him, and with him were eighty priests of the Lord—valiant men.

—2 Chronicles 26:16–17

Then Hezekiah humbled himself for the pride of his heart, he and the inhabitants of Jerusalem, so that the wrath of the LORD did not come upon them in the days of Hezekiah.

—2 Chronicles 32:26

The wicked in his proud countenance does not seek God; God is in none of his thoughts.

—Psalms 10:4

Therefore, pride serves as their necklace; Violence covers them like a garment.

—Psalms 73:6

The fear of the LORD is to hate evil; Pride and arrogance and the evil way, And the perverse mouth I hate.

—Proverbs 8:13

When pride comes, then comes shame; But with the humble is wisdom.

—Proverbs 11:2

In the mouth of a fool is a rod of pride, But the lips of the wise will preserve them.

—Proverbs 14:3

Pride goes before destruction, And a haughty spirit before a fall.

—Proverbs 16:18

...man's pride will bring him low, But the humble in spirit will retain honor.

—Proverbs 29:23

But when his heart was lifted up, and his spirit was hardened in pride, he was deposed from his kingly throne, and they took his glory from him.

—Daniel 5:20

When they had pasture, they were filled; They were filled, and their heart was exalted; Therefore, they forgot Me.

—Hosea 13:6

Then Jesus called a little child to Him, set him in the midst of them, and said, "Assuredly, I say to you, unless you are converted and become as little children, you will by no means enter the kingdom of heaven. Therefore, whoever humbles himself as this little child is the greatest in the kingdom of heaven."

—Matthew 18:2–4

...thefts, covetousness, wickedness, deceit, lewdness, an evil eye, blasphemy, pride, foolishness.

—Mark 7:22

And lest I should be exalted above measure by the abundance of the revelations, a thorn in the flesh was given to me, a messenger of Satan to buffet me, lest I be exalted above measure. Concerning this thing I pleaded with the Lord three times that it might depart from me. And He said to me, "My grace is sufficient for you, for My strength is made perfect in weakness." Therefore, most gladly I will rather boast in my infirmities, that the power of Christ may rest upon me. Therefore, I take pleasure in infirmities, in reproaches, in needs, in persecutions, in distresses, for Christ's sake. For when I am weak, then I am strong.

—2 Corinthians 12:7–10

because "All flesh is as grass, And all the glory of man as the flower of the grass. The grass withers, And its flower falls away

—1 Peter 1:24

For all that is in the world—the lust of the flesh, the lust of the eyes, and the pride of life—is not of the Father but is of the world.

—1 John 2:16

NOTES:

Repentance

- Repentance allows God to forgive our sins, restore, and reconcile us to Himself.
- Repentance is the first step those who do not know the Lord as Savior, must take in order to become members of the family of God.

Because your heart was tender, and you humbled yourself before God when you heard His words against this place and against its inhabitants, and you humbled yourself before Me, and you tore your clothes and wept before Me, I also have heard you," says the Lord.

—2 Chronicles 34:27

If he does not turn back, He will sharpen His sword; He bends His bow and makes it ready.

—Psalms 7:12

The sacrifices of God are a broken spirit, A broken and a contrite heart-- These, O God, You will not despise.

—Psalms 51:17

To the Lord our God belong mercy and forgiveness, though we have rebelled against Him.

—Daniel 9:9

But go and learn what this means: "I desire mercy and not sacrifice." For I did not come to call the righteous, but sinners, to repentance."

—Matthew 9:13

Or do you despise the riches of His goodness, forbearance, and longsuffering, not knowing that the goodness of God leads you to repentance?

—Romans 2:4

For godly sorrow produces repentance leading to salvation, not to be regretted; but the sorrow of the world produces death.

—2 Corinthians 7:10

if they fall away, to renew them again to repentance, since they crucify again for themselves the Son of God and put Him to an open shame.

—Hebrews 6:6

The Lord is not slack concerning His promise, as some count slackness, but is longsuffering toward us, not willing that any should perish but that all should come to repentance.

—2 Peter 3:9

NOTES:

Salvation

- Trusting in the redemptive work of Christ is the only way sinful mankind can be saved, reconciled to God, and their names written in the Lamb's Book of Life.
- The Lord is able to deliver and save His people from difficult circumstances here on earth.

And Moses said to the people, "Do not be afraid. Stand still and see the salvation of the Lord, which He will accomplish for you today. For the Egyptians whom you see today, you shall see again no more forever."

—Exodus 14:13

The God of my strength, in whom I will trust, My shield and the horn of my salvation, My stronghold and my refuge: My Savior, You save me from violence.

—2 Samuel 22:3

*The Lord is my light and my salvation; Whom shall, I fear?
The Lord is the strength of my life; of who shall I be afraid?*

—Psalms 27:1

*For God is my King from of old, working salvation in the
midst of the earth.*

—Psalms 74:12

*And it will be said in that day: "Behold, this is our God; We
have waited for Him, and He will save us. This is the Lord;
We have waited for Him; We will be glad and rejoice in His
salvation."*

—Isaiah 25:9

*"Nor is there salvation in any other, for there is no other
name under heaven given among men by which we must be
saved."*

—Acts 4:12

*For I am not ashamed of the gospel of Christ, for it is the
power of God to salvation for everyone who believes, for the
Jew first and also for the Greek.*

—Romans 1:16

For with the heart one believes unto righteousness, and with the mouth confession is made unto salvation.

—Romans 10:10

In Him you also trusted, after you heard the word of truth, the gospel of your salvation; in whom also, having believed, you were sealed with the Holy Spirit of promise

—Ephesians 1:13

For God did not appoint us to wrath, but to obtain salvation through our Lord Jesus Christ,

—1 Thessalonians 5:9

how shall we escape if we neglect so great a salvation, which at the first began to be spoken by the Lord, and was confirmed to us by those who heard Him

—Hebrews 2:3

And anyone not found written in the Book of Life was cast into the lake of fire.

—Revelation 20:15

NOTES:

Satan

- Satan is the enemy of the souls of humanity.
- His main objective is to keep humanity from accepting the redemptive work Christ accomplished on the cross.
- The Lord, through the Holy Spirit, has made us victorious over Satan.

And no wonder! For Satan himself transforms himself into an angel of light.

—2 Corinthians 11:14

Put on the whole armor of God, that you may be able to stand against the wiles of the devil. For we do not wrestle against flesh and blood, but against principalities, against powers, against the rulers of the darkness of this age, against spiritual hosts of wickedness in the heavenly places. Therefore, take up the whole armor of God, that you may be able to withstand in the evil day, and having done all, to stand.

Stand therefore, having girded your waist with truth, having put on the breastplate of righteousness, and having shod your feet with the preparation of the gospel of peace; above all, taking the shield of faith with which, you will be able to quench all the fiery darts of the wicked one. And take the helmet of salvation, and the sword of the Spirit, which is the word of God

—Ephesians 6:11–17

Therefore, submit to God. Resist the devil and he will flee from you.

—James 4:7

Be sober, be vigilant; because your adversary the devil walks about like a roaring lion, seeking whom he may devour. Resist him, steadfast in the faith, knowing that the same sufferings are experienced by your brotherhood in the world.

—1 Peter 5:8–9

So the great dragon was cast out, that serpent of old, called the Devil and Satan, who deceives the whole world; he was cast to the earth, and his angels were cast out with him.

—Revelation 12:9

He laid hold of the dragon, that serpent of old, who is the Devil and Satan, and bound him for a thousand years.

—Revelation 20:2

The devil, who deceived them, was cast into the lake of fire and brimstone where the beast and the false prophet are. And they will be tormented day and night forever and ever.

—Revelation 20:10

NOTES:

Sexual Sins

- Sexual sins, which include pornography, are works of the flesh and contrary to God-approved use of sexual intimacy.
- Sex outside God's plan is sinful and always leads to many painful results.
- God can forgive sexual sins and give a person complete cleansing and deliverance (see "Homosexuality").

...but that we write to them to abstain from things polluted by idols, from sexual immorality, from things strangled, and from blood.

—Acts 15:20

Likewise, also the men, leaving the natural use of the woman, burned in their lust for one another, men with men committing what is shameful, and receiving in themselves the penalty of their error which was due. And even as they did not like to retain God in their knowledge, God gave them over to a debased mind, to do those things which are not fitting.

—Romans 1:27–28

Do you not know that the unrighteous will not inherit the kingdom of God? Do not be deceived. Neither fornicators, nor idolaters, nor adulterers, nor homosexuals, nor sodomites, nor thieves, nor covetous, nor drunkards, nor revilers, nor extortioners will inherit the kingdom of God. And such were some of you. But you were washed, but you were sanctified, but you were justified in the name of the Lord Jesus and by the Spirit of our God. All things are lawful for me, but all things are not helpful. All things are lawful for me, but I will not be brought under the power of any. Foods for the stomach and the stomach for foods, but God will destroy both it and them. Now the body is not for sexual immorality but for the Lord, and the Lord for the body. And God both raised up the Lord and will also raise us up by His power. Do you not know that your bodies are members of Christ? Shall I then take the members of Christ and make them members of a harlot? Certainly not! Or do you not know that he who is joined to a harlot is one body with her? For "the two," He says, "shall become one flesh." But he who is joined to the Lord is one spirit with Him. Flee sexual immorality. Every sin that a man does is outside the body, but he who commits sexual immorality sins against his own body.

—1 Corinthians 6:9–18

Now the works of the flesh are evident, which are: adultery, fornication, uncleanness, lewdness,

—Galatians 5:19

But fornication and all uncleanness or covetousness, let it not even be named among you, as is fitting for saints

—Ephesians 5:3

For this is the will of God, your sanctification: that you should abstain from sexual immorality.

—1 Thessalonians 4:3

Marriage is honorable among all, and the bed undefiled; but fornicators and adulterers God will judge.

—Hebrews 13:4

NOTES:

Sickness

- Our God is still a healer contrary to what some false teachers say.
- God is able to heal our physical bodies as well as our spiritual infirmities (pathologies).
- Spiritual "sickness" is more deadly than physical sickness.

In those days Hezekiah was sick and near death. And Isaiah the prophet, the son of Amoz, went to him and said to him, "Thus says the LORD: 'Set your house in order, for you shall die, and not live.'" Then he turned his face toward the wall, and prayed to the LORD, saying, "Remember now, O LORD, I pray, how I have walked before You in truth and with a loyal heart and have done what was good in Your sight." And Hezekiah wept bitterly. And it happened, before Isaiah had gone out into the middle court, that the word of the LORD came to him, saying, "Return and tell Hezekiah the leader of My people, 'Thus says the LORD, the God of David your father: I have heard your prayer, I have seen your tears; surely, I will heal you. On the third day you shall go up to the house of the LORD.'"

—2 Kings 20:1-5

...that it might be fulfilled which was spoken by Isaiah the prophet, saying: "He Himself took our infirmities and bore our sicknesses."

—Matthew 8:17

Then Jesus went about all the cities and villages, teaching in their synagogues, preaching the gospel of the kingdom, and healing every sickness and every disease among the people.

—Matthew 9:35

But when the multitudes knew it, they followed Him; and He received them and spoke to them about the kingdom of God and healed those who had need of healing.

—Luke 9:11

And He said to me, "My grace is sufficient for you, for My strength is made perfect in weakness." Therefore, most gladly I will rather boast in my infirmities, that the power of Christ may rest upon me.

—2 Corinthians 12:9

Is anyone among you sick? Let him call for the elders of the church, and let them pray over him, anointing him with oil in the name of the Lord.

—James 5:14

And I heard a loud voice from heaven saying, "Behold, the tabernacle of God is with men, and He will dwell with them, and they shall be His people. God Himself will be with them and be their God. And God will wipe away every tear from their eyes; there shall be no more death, nor sorrow, nor crying. There shall be no more pain, for the former things have passed away."

—Revelation 21:3–4

NOTES:

Sin/Sinfulness

- All human beings are born in sin and subject to God's judgment.
- Therefore, all human beings need salvation through Christ to avoid eternal damnation.
- Believers who fall into sin can call on the Lord in repentance and He will forgive them.
- Spiritually healthy believers do not support or ignore sin/sinfulness in their own lives or in the lives of others.
- Tolerating sin, as a means to any end, confounds and diminishes our representation of Christ here on earth.

Remember, O Lord, your tender mercies and Your loving kindnesses, for they are from of old. Do not remember the sins of my youth, nor my transgressions; According to Your mercy remember me, For Your goodness' sake, O Lord. Good and up-right is the Lord; Therefore, He teaches sinners in the way.

—Psalms 25:6–8

Have mercy upon me, O God, According to Your lovingkindness;

According to the multitude of Your tender mercies, Blot out my transgressions. Wash me thoroughly from my iniquity,

And cleanse me from my sin. For I acknowledge my transgressions,

And my sin is always before me. Against You, you only, have I sinned,

And done this evil in Your sight—

That You may be found just when You speak, and blame-less when You judge. Behold, I was brought forth in iniquity, and in sin my mother conceived me.

—Psalms 51:1

For all have sinned and fall short of the glory of God,

—Romans 3:23

Therefore, just as through one man sin entered the world, and death through sin, and thus death spread to all men, be-cause all sinned—

—Romans 5:12

...knowing this, that our old man was crucified with Him, that the body of sin might be done away with, that we should no longer be slaves of sin. For he who has died has been freed from sin. Now if we died with Christ, we believe that we shall also live with Him, knowing that Christ, having been raised from the dead, dies no more. Death no longer has dominion over Him.

—Romans 6:6–9

...that you put off, concerning your former conduct, the old man which grows corrupt according to the deceitful lusts, and be renewed in the spirit of your mind, and that you put on the new man which was created according to God, in true righteousness and holiness.

—Ephesians 4:22–24

This is the message which we have heard from Him and declare to you, that God is light and in Him is no darkness at all. If we say that we have fellowship with Him, and walk in darkness, we lie and do not practice the truth. But if we walk in the light as He is in the light, we have fellowship with one another, and the blood of Jesus Christ His Son cleanses us from all sin. If we say that we have no sin, we deceive ourselves, and the truth is not in us. If we confess our sins, He is faithful and just to forgive us our sins and to cleanse us from all unrigh-

teousness. *If we say that we have not sinned, we make Him a liar, and His word is not in us.*

—1 John 1:5–10

NOTES:

Sorrow

- Experiencing sorrow is part of being human in a sinful world.
- But when, in our sorrow, we call on the Lord, He hears and responds to us.
- In the end, when the Lord returns for His people, He will wipe out all our tears and sorrows.

And the LORD said: "I have surely seen the oppression of My people who are in Egypt, and have heard their cry because of their taskmasters, for I know their sorrows."
—Exodus 3:7

"Do not consider your maidservant a wicked woman, for out of the abundance of my complaint and grief I have spoken until now."
—1 Samuel 1:16

Therefore, the king said to me, "Why is your face sad, since you are not sick? This is nothing but sorrow of heart." So, I became dreadfully afraid,

—Nehemiah 2:2

Then I would still have comfort; Though in anguish I would exult,

He will not spare; For I have not concealed the words of the Holy One.

—Job 6:10

My eye has also grown dim because of sorrow, and all my members are like shadows.

—Job 17:7

Strength dwells in his neck, And sorrow dances before him.

—Job 41:22

The days of our lives are seventy years; And if by reason of strength they are eighty years, yet their boast is only labor and sorrow; For it is soon cut off, and we fly away.

—Psalms 90:10

He will swallow up death forever, And the Lord God will wipe away tears from all faces; The rebuke of His people He will take away from all the earth; For the Lord has spoken.

—Isaiah 25:8

Look, all you who kindle a fire, Who encircle yourselves with sparks: Walk in the light of your fire and in the sparks you have kindled—This you shall have from My hand: You shall lie down in torment.

—Isaiah 50:11

He is despised and rejected by men, A Man of sorrows and acquainted with grief. And we hid, as it were, our faces from Him; He was despised, and we did not esteem Him.

—Isaiah 53:3

Blessed are those who mourn, for they shall be comforted.

—Matthew 5:4

Rejoice with those who rejoice, and weep with those who weep.

—Romans 12:15

...so that, on the contrary, you ought rather to forgive and comfort him, lest perhaps such a one be swallowed up with too much sorrow.

—2 Corinthians 2:7

But I do not want you to be ignorant, brethren, concerning those who have fallen asleep, lest you sorrow as others who have no hope.

—1 Thessalonians 4:13

And God will wipe away every tear from their eyes; there shall be no more death, nor sorrow, nor crying. There shall be no more pain, for the former things have passed away.

—Revelation 21:4

NOTES:

Stress/Suffering

- Stress and suffering are results of the fall of humanity in the Garden of Eden.
- Suffering and stress will remain the experience of humanity until the reign of Christ.
- However, the Lord has promised to be with us, His people, in our times of stress and suffering.

And those who know Your name will put their trust in You; For You, Lord, have not forsaken those who seek You.
—Psalms 9:10

My flesh and my heart fail; But God is the strength of my heart and my portion forever.
—Psalms 73:26

A thousand may fall at your side, and ten thousand at your right hand; But it shall not come near you. Only with your eyes shall you look and see the reward of the wicked. Because you have made the Lord, who is my refuge, Even the Most High, your dwelling place, No evil shall befall you, nor shall any plague come near your dwelling; For He shall give His angels charge over you, to keep you in all your ways.

—Psalms 91:7

For I consider that the sufferings of this present time are not worthy to be compared with the glory which shall be revealed in us. For the earnest expectation of the creation eagerly waits for the revealing of the sons of God. For the creation was subjected to futility, not willingly, but because of Him who subjected it in hope, because the creation itself also will be delivered from the bondage of corruption into the glorious liberty of the children of God.

—Romans 8:18–21

We are hard pressed on every side, yet not crushed; we are perplexed, but not in despair; persecuted, but not forsaken; struck down, but not destroyed —

—2 Corinthians 4:8–9

Be sober, be vigilant; because your adversary the devil walks about like a roaring lion, seeking whom he may devour. Resist him, steadfast in the faith, knowing that the same sufferings are experienced by your brotherhood in the world.

—1 Peter 5:8–9

NOTES:

Suicide

- During the extreme suffering in which Job (a servant of God) found himself, his wife recommended that he commit suicide.
- What Job needed was someone who would give him hope.
- Those contemplating suicide need reassurance that the God of Job is still on the throne, with abundant grace and mercy to deliver from self or Satan inflicted suffering.

Then his wife said to him, "Do you still hold fast to your integrity? Curse God and die!"

—Job 2:9

Do not withhold Your tender mercies from me, O Lord; Let Your lovingkindness and Your truth continually preserve me. For innumerable evils have surrounded me; My iniquities have overtaken me, so that I am not able to look up; They are more than the hairs of my head; Therefore, my heart fails me. Be pleased, O Lord, to deliver me; O Lord, make haste to help me!

—Psalms 40:11–13

Why are you cast down, O my soul? And why are you disquieted within me? Hope in God; For I shall yet praise Him, The help of my countenance and my God.

—Psalms 42:11

Why are you cast down, O my soul? And why are you disquieted within me? Hope in God; For I shall yet praise Him, The help of my countenance and my God.

—Psalms 43:5

"Ask, and it will be given to you; seek, and you will find; knock, and it will be opened to you. For everyone who asks receives, and he who seeks finds, and to him who knocks it will be opened. Or what man is there among you who, if his son asks for bread, will give him a stone? Or if he asks for a fish, will he give him a serpent? If you then, being evil, know how to give good gifts to your children, how much more will your Father who is in heaven give good things to those who ask Him!

—Matthew 7:7–11

The thief does not come except to steal, and to kill, and to destroy. I have come that they may have life, and that they may have it more abundantly.

—John 10:10

For whatever things were written before were written for our learning, that we through the patience and comfort of the Scriptures might have hope.

—Romans 15:4

Be anxious for nothing, but in everything by prayer and supplication, with thanksgiving, let your requests be made known to God; and the peace of God, which surpasses all understanding, will guard your hearts and minds through Christ Jesus. Finally, brethren, whatever things are true, whatever things are noble, whatever things are just, whatever things are pure, whatever things are lovely, whatever things are of good report, if there is any virtue and if there is anything praiseworthy--meditate on these things.

—Philippians 4:6–8

NOTES:

Temptation

- Exposure to temptation (by self, Satan, or others) is part of every believer's life.
- The Holy Spirit can help us to be victorious and escape sin.
- God will always make a way of escape from our temptations.
- The Lord is pleased when we do not fall into sin during temptation.

Then Jesus was led up by the Spirit into the wilderness to be tempted by the devil. And when He had fasted forty days and forty nights, afterward He was hungry. Now when the tempter came to Him, he said, "If You are the Son of God, command that these stones become bread." But He answered and said, "It is written, 'Man shall not live by bread alone, but by every word that proceeds from the mouth of God.'"

—Matthew 4:1–4

Immediately the Spirit drove Him into the wilderness. And He was there in the wilderness forty days, tempted by Satan, and was with the wild beasts; and the angels ministered to Him.

—Mark 1:12

No temptation has overtaken you except such as is common to man; but God is faithful, who will not allow you to be tempted beyond what you are able, but with the temptation will also make the way of escape, that you may be able to bear it.

—1 Corinthians 10:13

Brethren, if a man is overtaken in any trespass, you who are spiritual restore such a one in a spirit of gentleness, considering yourself lest you also be tempted.

—Galatians 6:1

For in that He Himself has suffered, being tempted, He is able to aid those who are tempted.

—Hebrews 2:18

For we do not have a High Priest who cannot sympathize with our weaknesses, but was in all points tempted as we are, yet without sin.

—Hebrews 4:15

My brethren, count it all joy when you fall into various trials, knowing that the testing of your faith produces patience. But let patience have its perfect work, that you may be perfect and complete, lacking nothing.

—James 1:2–4

Blessed is the man who endures temptation; for when he has been approved, he will receive the crown of life which the Lord has promised to those who love Him. Let no one say when he is tempted, "I am tempted by God"; for God cannot be tempted by evil, nor does He Himself tempt anyone. But each one is tempted when he is drawn away by his own desires and enticed.

—James 1:12-14

...and delivered righteous Lot, who was oppressed by the filthy conduct of the wicked (for that righteous man, dwelling among them, tormented his righteous soul from day to day by seeing and hearing their lawless deeds)— then the Lord knows how to deliver the godly out of temptations and to reserve the unjust under punishment for the day of judgment,

—2 Peter 2:7–9

NOTES:

Trusting God

- When earthly circumstances shake our faith in the Lord, we need to remember that our God is faithful, trustworthy, and does not change.
- He has never (and will never) failed those who trust in Him.

Therefore, know that the LORD your God, He is God, the faithful God who keeps covenant and mercy for a thousand generations with those who love Him and keep His commandments

—Deuteronomy 7:9

The God of my strength, in whom I will trust; My shield and the horn of my salvation, My stronghold and my refuge; My Savior, You save me from violence.

—2 Samuel 22:3

As for God, His way is perfect; The word of the Lord is proven; He is a shield to all who trust in Him.

—2 Samuel 22:31

He trusted in the Lord God of Israel, so that after him was none like him among all the kings of Judah, nor who were before him.

—2 Kings 18:5

And they were helped against them, and the Hagrites were delivered into their hand, and all who were with them, for they cried out to God in the battle. He heeded their prayer, because they put their trust in Him.

—1 Chronicles 5:20

Though He slay me, yet will I trust Him. Even so, I will defend my own ways before Him.

—Job 13:15

Although you say you do not see Him, yet justice is before Him, and you must wait for Him [trust thou in him].

—Job 35:14

Oh, how great is Your goodness, Which You have laid up for those who fear You, Which You have prepared for those who trust in You In the presence of the sons of men!

—Psalms 31:19

Commit your way to the Lord, trust also in Him, And He shall bring it to pass.

—Psalms 37:5

And the Lord shall help them and deliver them: he shall deliver them from the wicked, and save them, because they trust in him.

—Psalms 37:40

Whenever I am afraid, I will Trust in You...In God I have put my trust; I will not be afraid. What can man do to me?

—Psalms 56:3,11

Trust in him at all times; ye people, pour out your heart before him: God is a refuge for us. Selah.

—Psalms 62:8

It is better to trust in the Lord Than to put confidence in man. It is better to trust in the Lord Than to put confidence in princes.

— Psalm 118:9

Trust in the Lord with all your heart, and lean not on your own understanding.

—Proverbs 3:5

Every word of God is pure: he is a shield unto them that put their trust in him.

—Proverbs 30:5

The Lord is good, A stronghold in the day of trouble; And He knows those who trust in Him.

—Nahum 1:7

Yes, we had the sentence of death in ourselves, that we should not trust in ourselves but in God who raises the dead,

—2 Corinthians 1:9

For we walk by faith, not by sight.

—2 Corinthians 5:7

And again: "I will put My trust in Him." And again: "Here am I and the children whom God has given Me."

—Hebrews 2:13

Now the just shall live by faith; But if anyone draws back, My soul has no pleasure in him."

—Hebrews 10:38

But without faith it is impossible to please Him, for he who comes to God must believe that He is, and that He is a reward-er of those who diligently seek Him.

—Hebrews 11:6

NOTES:

Uncertainty/ The Future

- If we commit our future into the hands of the Lord, we can be certain that He will "direct our path" at all times.
- Faith and doubt cannot spiritually co-exist.
- He will protect us from confusion.

In thee, O Lord, do I put my trust let me never be put to confusion

—Psalms 71:1

Trust in the Lord with all your heart and lean not on your own understanding. In all your ways acknowledge Him and He shall direct your path.

—Proverbs 3:5-6

Therefore, I run thus: not with uncertainty. Thus, I fight not as one who beats the air.

—1 Corinthians 9:26

Let us hold fast the confession of our hope without wavering, for He who promised is faithful.

—Hebrews 10:23

But let him ask in faith, with no doubting, for he who doubts is like a wave of the sea driven and tossed by the wind. For let not that man suppose that he will receive anything from the Lord; he is a double-minded man, unstable in all his ways.

—James 1:6-8

NOTES:

Unity (Christian)

- The unity of God's people (Christians) is commanded in these verses to achieve and show the following:
- We love the Lord and one another.
- Our mission is to make Christ known to the world.
- We all share the same eternal destiny.
- We live and show a godly lifestyle to the world around us.
- Our unity should transcend our diversity and disunity.
- We are one in Christ.

Also the hand of God was on Judah to give them singleness of heart to obey the command of the king and the leaders, at the word of the LORD.

—2 Chronicles 30:12

Behold, how good and how pleasant it is For brethren to dwell together in unity!

—Psalms 133:1

But you, do not be called 'Rabbi'; for One is your Teacher, the Christ, and you are all brethren.

—Matthew 23:8

"By this all will know that you are My disciples, if you have love for one another."

—John 13:35

And the glory which You gave Me I have given them, that they may be one just as We are one: I in them, and You in Me; that they may be made perfect in one, and that the world may know that You have sent Me, and have loved them as You have loved Me.

—John 17:22–23

For as we have many members in one body, but all the members do not have the same function, so we, being many, are one body in Christ, and individually members of one another. Having then gifts differing according to the grace that is given to us, let us use them: if prophecy, let us prophesy in proportion to our faith.

—Romans 12:4–6

Be of the same mind toward one another. Do not set your mind on high things but associate with the humble. Do not be wise in your own opinion.

—Romans 12:16

God is faithful, by whom you were called into the fellowship of His Son, Jesus Christ our Lord. Now I plead with you, brethren, by the name of our Lord Jesus Christ, that you all speak the same thing, and that there be no divisions among you, but that you be perfectly joined together in the same mind and in the same judgment.

—1 Corinthians 1:9–10

For as the body is one and has many members, but all the members of that one body, being many, are one body, so also is Christ. For by one Spirit we were all baptized into one body— whether Jews or Greeks, whether slaves or free—and have all been made to drink into one Spirit.

—1 Corinthians 12:12–13

For you are all sons of God through faith in Christ Jesus. For as many of you as were baptized into Christ have put on Christ. There is neither Jew nor Greek, there is neither slave nor free, there is neither male nor female; for you are all one in Christ Jesus.

—Galatians 3:26–28

In Him we have redemption through His blood, the for-giveness of sins, according to the riches of His grace which He made to abound toward us in all wisdom and prudence, having made known to us the mystery of His will, according to His good pleasure which He purposed in Himself, that in the dispensation of the fullness of the times He might gather together in one all things in Christ, both which are in heaven and which are on earth—in Him.

—Ephesians 1:7

For He Himself is our peace, who has made both one, and has broken down the middle wall of separation, having abol-ished in His flesh the enmity, that is, the law of command-ments contained in ordinances, so as to create in Himself one new man from the two, thus making peace,

—Ephesians 2:14–15

I, therefore, the prisoner of the Lord, beseech you to walk worthy of the calling with which you were called, with all low-liness and gentleness, with longsuffering, bearing with one another in love, endeavoring to keep the unity of the Spirit in the bond of peace. There is one body and one Spirit, just as you were called in one hope of your calling. one Lord, one faith, one baptism; one God and Father of all, who is above all, and through all, and in you all.

—Ephesians 4:1–6

And He Himself gave some to be apostles, some prophets, some evangelists, and some pastors and teachers, for the equipping of the saints for the work of ministry, for the edifying of the body of Christ, till we all come to the unity of the faith and of the knowledge of the Son of God, to a perfect man, to the measure of the stature of the fullness of Christ; from whom the whole body, joined and knit together by what every joint supplies, according to the effective working by which every part does its share, causes growth of the body for the edifying of itself in love.

—Ephesians 4:11–13,16

Therefore if there is any consolation in Christ, if any comfort of love, if any fellowship of the Spirit, if any affection and mercy, fulfill my joy by being like-minded, having the same love, being of one accord, of one mind. Let nothing be done through selfish ambition or conceit, but in lowliness of mind let each esteem others better than himself.

—Philippians 2:1–3

...bearing with one another, and forgiving one another, if anyone has a complaint against another; even as Christ forgave you, so you also must do. But above all these things put on love, which is the bond of perfection.

—Colossians 3:13–14

NOTES:

Vengeance

- A powerful way for a believer "to lift Christ up so He can draw people unto Himself" is to love and forgive those who do evil things to us.
- The Lord's Vengeance on our behalf is always perfect, while ours is imperfect because we are sinful and always in need of God's forgiveness.
- Should it happen that the person who wronged us goes to the Lord and asks for forgiveness because of what they did to us, the Lord can forgive him/her. Then our vengeance against the person will become spiritually impotent.
- The Lord is always on the side of those He has forgiven.

"You have heard that it was said, 'An eye for an eye and a tooth for a tooth.' But I tell you not to resist an evil person. But whoever slaps you on your right cheek, turn the other to him also. If anyone wants to sue you and take away your tunic, let

him have your cloak also. And whoever compels you to go one mile, go with him two. Give to him who asks you, and from him who wants to borrow from you do not turn away. You have heard that it was said, 'You shall love your neighbor and hate your enemy.' But I say to you, love your enemies, bless those who curse you, do good to those who hate you, and pray for those who spitefully use you and persecute you, that you may be sons of your Father in heaven; for He makes His sun rise on the evil and on the good and sends rain on the just and on the unjust. For if you love those who love you, what reward have you? Do not even the tax collectors do the same? And if you greet your brethren only, what do you do more than others? Do not even the tax collectors do so? Therefore, you shall be perfect, just as your Father in heaven is perfect."

—Matthew 5:38–48

And we know that all things work together for good to those who love God, to those who are the called according to His purpose.

—Romans 8:28

Repay no one evil for evil. Have regard for good things in the sight of all men. If it is possible, as much as depends on you, live peaceably with all men. Beloved do not avenge yourselves, but rather give place to wrath; for it is written, "Vengeance is Mine, I will repay," says the Lord. Therefore "If your *enemy is hungry, feed him; If he is thirsty, give him a drink; For in so doing you will heap coals of fire on his head." Do not be overcome by evil but overcome evil with good.*

—Romans 12:17–21

Let all bitterness, wrath, anger, clamor, and evil speaking be put away from you, with all malice.

—Ephesians 4:31

And walk in love, as Christ also has loved us and given Himself for us, an offering and a sacrifice to God for a sweet-smelling aroma.

—Ephesians 5:2

NOTES:

Will of God

- Our lives as believers, glorify God when we live in His will for us.
- It, therefore, should be the supreme desire of each believer to seek the will of God for his/her life.
- We must always challenge others to seek and follow God's will for their lives.

Blessed is the man Who walks not in the counsel of the ungodly, nor stands in the path of sinners, nor sits in the seat of the scornful; But his delight is in the law of the Lord, And in His law he meditates day and night.

—Psalms 1:1–2

For whosoever shall do the will of my Father which is in heaven, the same is my brother, and sister, and mother.

—Matthew 12:50

For the Father loves the Son and shows Him all things that He Himself does; and He will show Him greater works than these, that you may marvel.

—John 5:20

These things He said, and after that He said to them, "Our friend Lazarus sleeps, but I go that I may wake him up."

—John 11:11

He will glorify Me, for He will take of what is Mine and declare it to you.

—John 16:14

For David, after he had served his own generation by the will of God, fell on sleep, and was laid unto his fathers, and saw corruption:

—Acts 13: 36

And when he would not be persuaded, we ceased, saying, the will of the Lord be done.

—Acts 21:14

For I am not ashamed of the gospel of Christ, for it is the power of God to salvation for everyone who believes, for the Jew first and also for the Greek.

—Romans 1:16

I beseech you therefore, brethren, by the mercies of God, that you present your bodies a living sacrifice, holy, acceptable to God, which is your reasonable service. And do not be conformed to this world, but be transformed by the renewing of your mind, that you may prove what is that good and acceptable and perfect will of God.

—Romans 12:1–2

Therefore, whether you eat or drink, or whatever you do, do all to the glory of God.

—1 Corinthians 10:31

I, therefore, the prisoner of the Lord, beseech you to walk worthy of the calling with which you were called,

—Ephesians 4:1

Wherefore be ye not unwise but understanding what the will of the Lord is.

—Ephesians 5:17

For this reason we also, since the day we heard it, do not cease to pray for you, and to ask that you may be filled with the knowledge of His will in all wisdom and spiritual understanding; that you may walk worthy of the Lord, fully pleasing Him, being fruitful in every good work and increasing in the knowledge of God; strengthened with all might, according to His glorious power, for all patience and longsuffering with joy; giving thanks to the Father who has qualified us to be partakers of the inheritance of the saints in the light.

—Colossians 1:9

But you have carefully followed my doctrine, manner of life, purpose, faith, longsuffering, love, perseverance, persecutions, afflictions, which happened to me at Antioch, at Iconium, at Lystra--what persecutions I endured. And out of them all the Lord delivered me. Yes, and all who desire to live godly in Christ Jesus will suffer persecution.

—2 Timothy 3:10

that which we have seen and heard we declare to you, that you also may have fellowship with us; and truly our fellowship is with the Father and with His Son Jesus Christ.

—1 John 1:3

NOTES:

Witnessing (Evangelism)

- These are useful verses for encouraging other believers to share their faith in Christ.
- They are also good reminders that the job of evangelism and soul-winning was given to us by Christ.
- We should, therefore, never be ashamed of the gospel.
- The Lord is always with us when we faithfully "lift Him up so He can draw men unto Himself"
- We always need the power of the Holy Spirit to be effective witnesses for Christ.

"Yet now be strong, Zerubbabel," says the LORD; "and be strong, Joshua, son of Jehozadak, the high priest; and be

strong, all you people of the land," says the LORD, "and work; for I am with you," says the LORD of hosts.

—Haggai 2:4

"No one can serve two masters; for either he will hate the one and love the other, or else he will be loyal to the one and despise the other. You cannot serve God and mammon."

—Matthew 6:24

Go therefore and make disciples of all the nations, baptizing them in the name of the Father and of the Son and of the Holy Spirit, teaching them to observe all things that I have commanded you; and lo, I am with you always, even to the end of the age." Amen.

—Matthew 28:19–20

"Most assuredly, I say to you, he who believes in Me, the works that I do he will do also; and greater works than these he will do, because I go to My Father."

—John 14:12

"I am the true vine, and My Father is the vinedresser. Every branch in Me that does not bear fruit He takes away; and every branch that bears fruit He prunes, that it may bear more fruit. You are already clean because of the word which I have spoken to you. Abide in Me, and I in you. As the branch cannot *bear fruit of itself, unless it abides in the vine, neither can you, unless you abide in Me. I am the vine; you are the branches. He who abides in Me, and I in him, bears much fruit; for without Me you can do nothing."*

—John 15:1-5

And He said to them, "It is not for you to know times or seasons which the Father has put in His own authority. But you shall receive power when the Holy Spirit has come upon you; and you shall be witnesses to Me in Jerusalem, and in all Judea and Samaria, and to the end of the earth."

—Acts 1:7–8

For I am not ashamed of the gospel of Christ, for it is the power of God to salvation for everyone who believes, for the Jew first and also for the Greek.

—Romans 1:16

For by grace you have been saved through faith, and that not of yourselves; it is the gift of God, not of works, lest anyone should boast.

—Ephesians 2:8–9

And be kind to one another, tenderhearted, forgiving one another, just as God in Christ forgave you.

—Ephesians 4:32

And you, who once were alienated and enemies in your mind by wicked works, yet now He has reconciled

—Colossians 1:21

And whatever you do, do it heartily, as to the Lord and not to men,

—Colossians 3:23

For the grace of God that brings salvation has appeared to all men,

—Titus 2:11

But when the kindness and the love of God our Savior toward man appeared, not by works of righteousness which we have done, but according to His mercy He saved us, through the washing of regeneration and renewing of the Holy Spirit, whom He poured out on us abundantly through Jesus Christ our Savior, that having been justified by His grace we should become heirs according to the hope of eternal life.

—Titus 3:4–7

I write to you, little children, because your sins are forgiven you for His name's sake.

—1 John 2:12

Beloved, while I was very diligent to write to you concerning our common salvation, I found it necessary to write to you exhorting you to contend earnestly for the faith which was once for all delivered to the saints.

—Jude 1:3

NOTES:

Worldliness

- Believers must always examine themselves and their lifestyle to ensure they are not driven by worldliness as described in these verses.
- We are called to be like Christ, not like the people of this sinful world.

"No one can serve two masters; for either he will hate the one and love the other, or else he will be loyal to the one and despise the other. You cannot serve God and mammon."
—Matthew 6:24

For what profit is it to a man if he gains the whole world, and loses his own soul? Or what will a man give in exchange for his soul?
—Matthew 16:26

Now these are the ones sown among thorns; they are the ones who hear the word, and the cares of this world, the de-

ceitfulness of riches, and the desires for other things entering in choke the word, and it becomes unfruitful. But these are the ones sown on good ground, those who hear the word, accept it, and bear fruit: some thirtyfold, some sixty, and some a hundred.

—Mark 4:18–20

I beseech you therefore, brethren, by the mercies of God, that you present your bodies a living sacrifice, holy, acceptable to God, which is your reasonable service. And do not be conformed to this world, but be transformed by the renewing of your mind, that you may prove what is that good and acceptable and perfect will of God.

—Romans 12:1–2

Therefore, I urge you, imitate me.

—1 Corinthians 4:16

Set your mind on things above, not on things on the earth.

—Colossians 3:2

Do not be unequally yoked together with unbelievers. For what fellowship has righteousness with lawlessness? And what communion has light with darkness? And what accord has Christ with Belial? Or what part has a believer with an unbeliever? And what agreement has the temple of God with idols? For you are the temple of the living God.

—2 Corinthians 6:14-16

And you became followers of us and of the Lord, having received the word in much affliction, with joy of the Holy Spirit,

—1 Thessalonians 1:6

Adulterers and adulteresses! Do you not know that friendship with the world is enmity with God? Whoever therefore wants to be a friend of the world makes himself an enemy of God.

—James 4:4

Do not love the world or the things in the world. If anyone loves the world, the love of the Father is not in him. For all that is in the world--the lust of the flesh, the lust of the eyes, and the pride of life--is not of the Father but is of the world. And the world is passing away, and the lust of it; but he who does the will of God abides forever.

—1 John 2:15

Beloved, do not imitate what is evil, but what is good. He who does good is of God, but he who does evil has not seen God.

—3 John 1:11

NOTES: